BAKER STUDIES IN BIBLICAL ARCHAEOLOGY

D0933332

JERUSALEM
A STUDY IN URBAN GEOGRAPHY

BAKER STUDIES IN BIBLICAL ARCHAEOLOGY

JERUSALEM

A STUDY IN URBAN GEOGRAPHY

by

I. W. J. Hopkins

BAKER BOOK HOUSE
Grand Rapids, Michigan

Standard Book Number: 8010-4000-0
Library of Congress Catalog Card Number: 76-101615

Printed in the United States of America

PREFACE

Jerusalem, as a holy city for three great religions of the world, is a city known superficially by millions. Archaeologists and Biblical scholars have attempted to reconstruct the city as it was before its destruction in A.D. 70; and historians of the Arab world have brought out its significance in Middle East history since that date. In this study an attempt is made to examine the city from a different angle — that of the geographer. The city is "taken apart" and examined from different angles, in the same way that other cities have been studied in the past few decades. The material here has been presented in the usual pattern developed by urban geographers, i.e. site; function; and morphology. However, as the reader will soon appreciate, the nature of this city makes it almost as much a microcosmic study in the geography of religion as a traditional urban geography.

Field work on Jerusalem was undertaken in 1965 and 1968, in the first instance supported by the Central Research Fund of London University, and in the second instance by the Centre for Middle Eastern and Islamic Studies, University of Durham. I would like to thank many friends in Jerusalem for their assistance, particularly Professor Y. Karmon of the Department of Geography in the Hebrew University, Canon Edward Every of St. George's Cathedral, and Rev. Salem Dawani now in Salt, Jordan. Thanks are also due to my former colleagues in the University of Durham for assistance with ad hoc problems and particularly to my wife for her professional assistance with statistical problems and help in reading manuscript and proofs. Nevertheless, any errors or strange opinions expressed herein are entirely the author's. Finally, the author would like to express his appreciation to Mr. Cornelius Zylstra and Mr. Gordon De Young of Baker Book House for their patient and helpful editorial work.

No attempt is made in this study to deal at length with the problems attached to the authenticity of the many holy sites; nevertheless it is hoped that it will throw some new light on the city's physical development and geographical character which will be of help both to Bible students and to those interested in the modern problems of the Holy Land.

IAN W. J. HOPKINS

Stoke Holy Cross,
Norwich, England

ILLUSTRATIONS

CONTENTS

JERUSALEM

.... Relief Form Lines

.... Streets Demolished since 1967

✛ Christian Churches and Sites

∪ Moslem Sites

✽ Jewish Sites

◆ Site Shared by All Faiths

PLACES
A Holy Sepulcher Church
B Dome of the Rock
C Al Aqsa Mosque

D Church of the Redeemer
E Church of St. John the Baptist
F Christ Church
G Syrian Orthodox Church
H St. James's Church

STREETS
1 Suq Khan es-zeit
2 David Street
3 Via Dolorosa
4 St. Francis Street
5 Street of the Chain
6 Nablus Road
7 Saladin Street
8 Jaffa Road
9 Shlomzion Hamalka
10 Bethlehem Road

Mosque

New Gate

Jaffa Gate

Muristan

Citadel

YEMIN MOSHE

Zion Gate

Dormition

MOUNT SION

◆ Coenaculum

St. ✛ Andrew's

HINNOM VALLEY

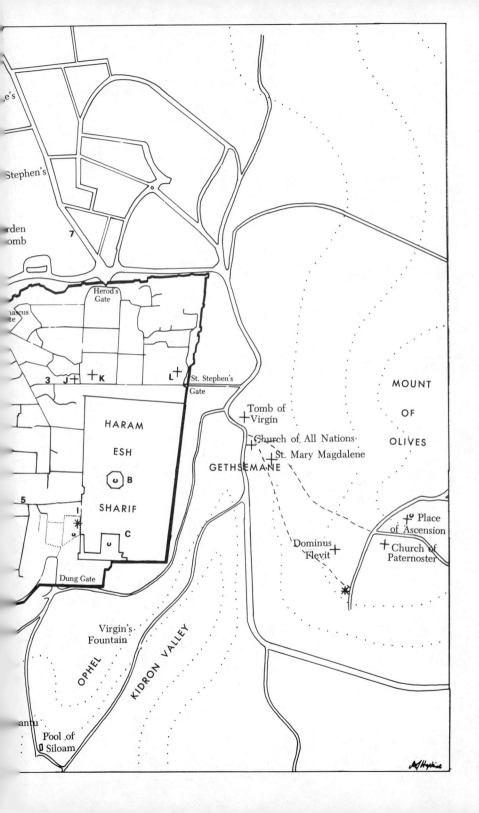

I

THE CITY IN ITS REGIONAL SETTING

In the Middle Ages, cartographers drew their world maps with Jerusalem at the center and although their reasons for this were spiritual rather than scientific, they were nearer the truth than they have been given credit for. In many respects the land we know as Palestine is a crucial physical and cultural part of the globe, situated as it is at the heart of the Middle East, which has often been called the crossroads of the world. Here East and West have for many centuries found a common meeting point for the exchange of goods and ideas, and from time to time to shed blood in conflict for this small tract of land. Palestine has been the highway for invading armies from either end of the "Fertile Crescent," that strip of relatively cultivable land sandwiched between the desert on one hand, and the sea and mountains of Asia Minor on the other. From the Nile Valley or Mesopotamia, armies have marched along its north-south highways; bedouin hordes have encroached on its desert frontiers in the east; and invaders arrived by sea from the west, whether Philistines, Romans, Crusaders or Zionist Jews. The Psalmist described the city of Jerusalem, perched on the hills in the middle of this land, as "beautiful in elevation, the joy of the whole earth" (Ps. 48:2). Palestine has time and again held the attention of world opinion and been the center of men's hopes and aspirations.

Yet the city of Jerusalem which is the capital and focus of the people of Palestine, is in many respects "off the beaten track," and a long way from being the hub of this crossroads of the Middle East. It lies to the east of the water-parting of the central range of hills, hidden from the main international route which traverses the coastal plain, while to the east it faces di-

11

rectly onto the desert, the Wilderness of Judea, with the dark cliffs of Moab and Ammon seeming very close across the Jordan and the Dead Sea. Jerusalem is a minor crossroads of two routes which serve the local population, but neither route has ever carried a large volume of international traffic. As we shall see, it owes its existence largely to its excellent defenses, its centrality to the Hill Country tribes and to the great religious significance which it has held ever since Solomon built his temple there. As a commercial center it has generally had to give place to cities on the coastal plain. However, this relative isolation has been the saving of Jerusalem in the past and the invading empires from Mesopotamia or the Nile have often found it not worth capturing at a great cost. It has often been regarded as too insignificant in military terms and too far off the main commercial highways, and before the invention of the airplane access to it was very difficult.

Thus Jerusalem has played a dual role in this ancient land. Although in many respects a world city, receiving pilgrims from all nations, often the capital of Palestine, always the spiritual goal of Christianity and Judaism, it has generally remained a small city and out of the mainstream of commercial life. The Arabs never made it an imperial capital despite its sacred character to Moslems; the Israelis have held it as capital, but the commercial heart of Israel is Tel Aviv. However, this has all helped to preserve Jerusalem and to give it an appeal which continues to attract tourists and pilgrims from all over the world.

THE SETTING OF JERUSALEM

In discussing the physical environs of a city, geographers distinguish between the site of the city, its immediate natural landscape and the hills and valleys on which it is built, and the "situation" of the city — its position in terms of the country or region of which it is part. In this chapter we are concerned with the situation of Jerusalem and will therefore discuss the region around the city and assess the relationship between Jerusalem and the towns and villages within that region.[1]

The land of Palestine lies in a narrow stretch of the Fertile Crescent at the southern end of the Levantine coast. It is really very narrow in east-west extent and this narrowness is accentuated by the main physical divisions of the area which run

---

1 See also E. Orni and E. Efrat, *Geography of Israel*, pp. 49-69; and D. Baly, *Geography of the Bible*, Ch. XIV.

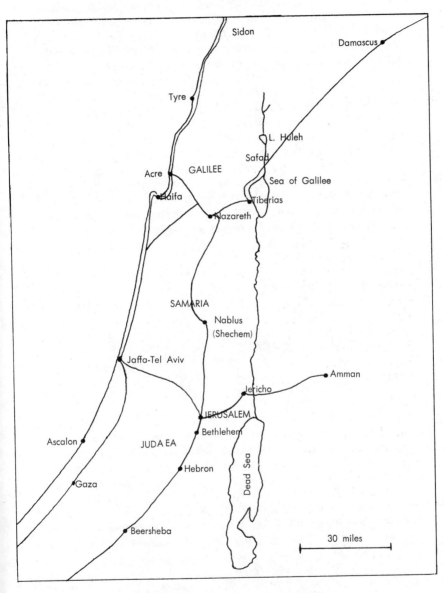

Palestine: **MAIN TOWNS & ROUTES**

in a north-south direction. The desert is never very far away to the east and from time to time has encroached on more fertile land either because of fluctuations in climate or the raids of the desert nomads which have destroyed many a frontier settlement. The Mediterranean Sea to the west has brought both traders and raiders, while to the north communications are impeded by the mountains of Lebanon. To the south are the empty deserts of the Negev and Sinai. Within these borders, Palestine can be divided into four main strips of terrain.

To the west is the coastal plain, narrow north of Mount Carmel, but much wider further south. The coast itself has no good natural harbor and for most of its history, Joppa has been the main port, but in Roman times a new port was constructed called Caesarea. Today the main port is Haifa. The more fertile land east of the coastal sand dune belt has been more thickly settled, although much of Sharon, which lies between Tel Aviv-Jaffa and the Carmel Hills, was marsh until the settlement of the area by Jews in this century.

East of the coastal plain lies the second physical division of the land, the Hill Country. Here we have a line of limestone hills extending from the Lebanon Range to the Negev, broken into two by the Plain of Esdraelon. North of this plain are the hills of Galilee, rugged and wetter than those further south, which have been frequently invaded; but in their many valleys refuge has been found by small minority communities of Jews, Christians and Druzes. Now it is one of the most important parts of the State of Israel. South of Esdraelon lies the backbone of Palestine, the limestone hills of Samaria and Judea, flanked by the lower hills of the Shephelah to the west and the Wilderness to the east. These hills were the real homeland of the Jewish people in ancient times, although the Zionist settlements of recent decades generally avoided them and at the present time the villages are solidly Arab except in the Jerusalem corridor. It is these hill villages that have the strongest ties with the city of Jerusalem, depending on it as their main urban center. The whole region has often been in isolation from the rest of the country, a fact which is very noticeable in both cultural and economic characteristics.

East of the Hill Country lies the dramatic rift valley of the Jordan, so far below sea level that it has tropical temperatures all year round. It also has a wild and rugged scenery all its own in the "badlands" on either side of the river, and although the Jordan itself is not very large, the valley has often served as a strong barrier to movement and has frequently served as an in-

MT. ZION, as seen from the Hill of Offense. Courtesy, Levant Photo Service.

ternational border. Jericho is the main settlement in the valley and has had strong ties with Jerusalem, with which it is linked by a winding mountain road.

Beyond the Jordan are the rugged hills of Transjordan, facing the Judean hills in a steep scarp which can be plainly visible from the Mount of Olives on a clear day. Beyond the scarp lies the plateau, a relatively fertile area which holds many villages and towns. Still farther east is the desert where there is little permanent settlement and out of which tribes of nomads have frequently descended on the settled land.

The Jerusalem Region

Jerusalem has had relationships with all these regions of Palestine, although with the desert and the coastal plain these have been rather limited. The real region of the city, the area which is linked most closely with Jerusalem as a source of food and a market for manufactured goods, is much more confined. Throughout most of history it has consisted only of the hill regions of Judea and Samaria. At times, Jerusalem has acted as the capital of the whole of Palestine or even a larger area, but it is not well suited to such a task. Although centrally placed in physical terms, it is not central in social terms, for the main trunk route from the Nile valley to Mesopotamia passes along the coastal plain and through the Esdraelon valley, and there are no easy lines of communication into the hills and leading to the city.

The usual theories concerning city regions and central places tend to break down in Palestine.[2] Jerusalem has usually been the central place of Western Palestine between the Negev and Esdraelon, but links with places beyond are more tenuous. Immediately around the city there is a zone of several villages such as Eziriya, Beit Hanina and Anata, which benefit from proximity to it and supply food and additional labor. Beyond are two small towns, Bethlehem and Ramallah, themselves surrounded by further villages and acting as small market centers. On the fringe of the Jerusalem region are larger towns that serve a considerable local population — Nablus, Hebron, Beth Shemesh and Jericho. The whole area tends to be linked strongly with Jerusalem, using the city as a market center and an administrative center, as well as relying on it for a supply of tourists, or in former days, pilgrims. The lack of hotels and other tourist facilities in the surrounding towns and villages makes Jerusalem the main source of pilgrims and tourists to Samaria, Hebron, Bethlehem and other places of interest. As we shall see later, this tourist industry is of vital importance to the city and its environs and gives the whole region a unity and common economic interest.

Jerusalem's situation in relation to the rest of Palestine will now be further examined in detail by examining the four main axes of interdependency which connect the city with the surrounding cities. An axis of interdependency expresses the relationship between communities in terms of economic and social links between them, i.e. marketing, retailing, administration, recreation, etc. In general, these axes are followed by routes between the places on them, but while an axis, as expressed by a straight line, is constant and expresses a relationship rather than a topographical feature, a routeway takes a varied course

---

2 For a brief analysis of central-place theory, see P. Haggett, *Locational Analysis in Human Geography*, Ch. 5.

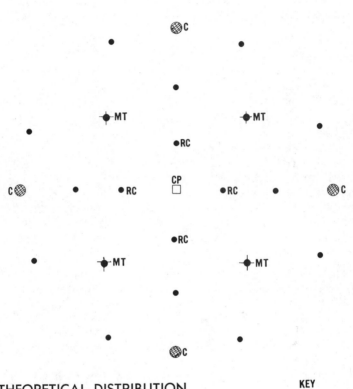

THEORETICAL DISTRIBUTION
OF URBAN CENTERS
(Simplified)

KEY

CP CENTRAL PLACE
RC RURAL CENTER
MT MARKET TOWN
 C CITY

and is liable to change in course of time as a result of war, technological change or physical controls.[3] The four axes out of Jerusalem are:

(1) To the north: linking Ramallah-Bireh, Nablus-Shechem, and ultimately Jenin, Nazareth and so to Damascus.

(2) To the south: linking Bethlehem, Hebron, Beersheba and ultimately Sinai.

(3)   To the west: linking Beth Shemesh, Ramleh, and Tel Aviv-Jaffa, having crossed the main international axis between the Nile and the Euphrates.

(4) To the east: linking Jericho, Salt, Amman and reaching the "King's Highway" route on the edge of the desert.

These axes are reflected in the two main routeways which intersect at Jerusalem, i.e. the hill crest route, following the water-parting of the hills and the east-west route from Transjordan, passing north of the Dead Sea and then on to the Mediterranean at Jaffa. Until recently, of course, political differences between Israel and Jordan considerably modified this pattern.

THE NORTHERN AXIS

The northern axis links Jerusalem with the villages and towns of the northern part of the Hill Country known as Samaria, and ultimately with Galilee and Syria. In pre-Exilic times it was the line of communication between the Judean capital and the kingdom of Israel, although communications between the two states were not always sufficiently close to enable strong commercial links to develop.

Between Jerusalem and the twin towns of Ramallah-Bireh is comparatively gentle rolling country with low hills and shallow valleys, and the elevation rises gradually as one travels from Jerusalem. Ramallah and Bireh occupy the sides of a col or pass in the mountain chain between two valleys. The area between Jerusalem and Ramallah-Bireh is covered with villages and there is today considerable ribbon development along the road between Jerusalem and Beit Hanina. The villages here are closely connected with Jerusalem, serving it with goods and buying in the suq of the city, but many are surprisingly isolated and backward. The social and economic gulf between city and country is much greater in the Middle East than in Western coun-

---

3 Israel Physical Master Plan: Jerusalem Region.

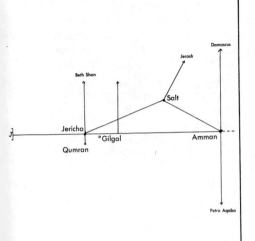

THE EASTERN AXIS

o Abandoned Settlements

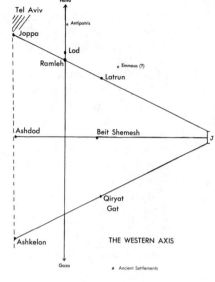

THE WESTERN AXIS

o Ancient Settlements

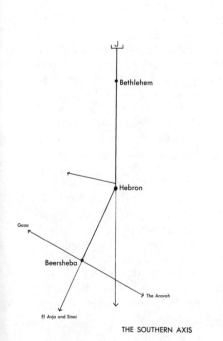

THE SOUTHERN AXIS

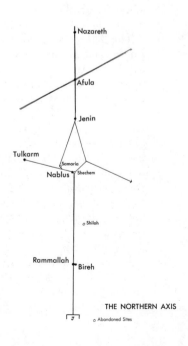

THE NORTHERN AXIS

o Abandoned Sites

tries. Apart from the present large number of settlements, there are many ruins which testify to a large population in the past and a number of Biblical names are perpetuated in the contemporary nomenclature, such as Al Jib (Gibeon), Ar Ram (Ramah) and Mukhmas (Michmash).

The fairly thick population of this area has provided Jerusalem with quite a prosperous northern environs, although the value of this in ancient times must have been limited by the border between the two Jewish states, which ran just north of the city. Immediately to the north of Jerusalem is the suburb of Sheik Jarrah which includes a number of hotels, but then beyond there is open country for a little way until the village of Shu'fat is reached. To the east is the village of Anata (Anathoth), beyond Mount Scopus, and further along the road is Beit Hanina. Nebi Samwil to the west is traditionally the birthplace of Samuel. Many of these villages have benefited in the past from their Biblical connections (real or imaginary) by the visits of pilgrims, and today most of them are within easy reach of Jerusalem. However, it should be emphasized that the primary means of subsistence in all of them is agriculture. While flocks of sheep or goats graze on the hillsides, picking out the patches of green among the rocks, the valleys are cultivated near the villages. The villages themselves are frequently located on hill tops or slopes, partly for defensive reasons and in part to keep the valleys clear for cultivation.

The first urban settlement reached in this direction is Ramallah-Bireh. Ramallah is a Christian town of relatively recent origin, but Bireh is considered to be on the site of ancient Beroth. It was here, according to tradition, that the events of Luke 2:44 took place, when Jesus was missed by his parents. It is a likely spot, being a stopping place on the hill crest route and probably served as a halting place for the caravans using this road out of Jerusalem. Ramallah has a soap factory today and is important as a summer resort because of its altitude, and so has a number of hotels. It provides a small market center for surrounding villages. From Ramallah, routes lead westward to serve a number of Hill Country villages and the western hills and valleys of this part of the mountain range are thickly settled.

About three miles north of Ramallah, the present road descends into the head of the valley of the Wadi Sarida, which although scenically attractive, was once very dangerous on account of the bandits who lurked there to attack travelers. Small watchtowers can be seen, built to protect local inhabitants and their crops. Only in this century has the valley been made safe, and this barrier has prevented frequent communication between Jerusalem and the towns of Samaria. There are several important villages in this area, such as Bir Zeit, Yabrud and Jiljiliya, and the land is quite thickly planted with trees. With a fairly high rainfall, this part of the Hill Country was always thickly settled when security was good enough and it was the "heartland" of the tribe of Ephraim. Beitin (Bethel) and other sites of Biblical interest abound.

Just to the north of the upper Sarida valley, where the road runs on more open ground again, the valley of Shilo is reached, with the ancient sanctuary a few miles east of the present road. Until Jerusalem was captured by David, Shilo was the central town and sanctuary of Israel and it was here that Eli ministered. It was far inferior to Jerusalem, however, and it is interesting to note that gatherings of the tribes tended to take place elsewhere, for example at Mizpeh (I Sam. 10:18) or Gilgal (I Sam. 11:14). This region has had fewer contacts with Jerusalem than that to the south of the Sarida valley and has frequently been separated from it by political divisions. In matters of commerce and administration the villages from Shilo northward have tended to look to Shechem, Samaria, or Nablus as a center rather than Jerusalem; so the immediate region of the city extends only as far as the Sarida in this direction.

The area of Samaria has never supported a city as large or illustrious as Jerusalem, but it has not been entirely lacking in urban growth. First Shechem grew up in the pass between Mt. Ebal and Mt. Gerizim, not far from Jacob's Well. It was at a natural junction of routes and well placed to serve as a market town for the many villages of this relatively prosperous district. Later it was supplanted by the city of Samaria, built west of the pass and in a good defensive point on a spur commanding the approach to the pass from the west. It was built as a royal city for the kings of Israel but was rejuvenated by Herod the Great who built on the site a Greek city called Sebaste. However, the urban center is now at Nablus, which lies in the center of the pass between Ebal and Gerizim and has flourished on its soap factories and flour mills. It is in many respects more of an agricultural center than Jerusalem and is not much smaller than the Arab sector of the holy city. Nablus has few tourist attractions apart from its small Samaritan community, but its rich farming environs make it less subject than Jerusalem to the fluctuations of international politics and finance which tend to make tourism an uncertain industry.

Beyond the town of Jenin, which lies where the Hill Country

gives way to the Esdraelon valley, is Galilee, the region with perhaps least contact with Jerusalem of all areas of Palestine. Among its hills and valleys are a large number of towns and villages, many of them steeped in Christian and Jewish tradition. Yet Galilee is much more open to outside influences than the hills of Judea. It is crossed by the international routeway, so its population is very mixed. The scorn with which the Jewish leaders greeted the teachings of Jesus of Nazareth shows the contempt felt by Jerusalemites for the inhabitants of this distant region. It is rather ironic that in latter days it has become one of the most important regions of the State of Israel.

THE SOUTHERN AXIS

Jerusalem has had strong connections with the region to the south of the city, although its influence has never really extended very far into the Negev. Consequently the axis to the south is considerably shorter than that to the north, but is probably stronger. The southern part of the Hill Country is not as rich as that north of Jerusalem largely on account of the paucity of rainfall, and for that reason the number of villages is less. There are a few springs and several large pools, and it is from this source that Jerusalem has obtained its auxiliary supplies of water until recent years. Solomon's Pools, although probably to be associated with Pilate rather than the son of King David, have given Jerusalem a very close tie with this part of the Hill Country. The axis finds expression in a very ancient routeway to Hebron, and it will be recalled that Abraham and the patriarchs moved along it in their migrations.

Only a few miles south of Jerusalem, Bethlehem is probably the town most dependent on it. With the Church of the Nativity and other associations with the birth of Christ, this town has always been a strong center for Christian pilgrimages, and it is still included in the itinerary of practically every visitor to Jerusalem. Bethlehem is also of interest to Jews as the city of David and the scene of the events in the Book of Ruth. It is largely a Christian town and, together with Beit Jala and Beit Sahur, is the nucleus of a small ring of settlements on the southern side of Jerusalem. The regular bus service between Bethlehem and Jerusalem is an indication of the close links between the two places. Many of the mother-of-pearl and the olive wood souvenirs sold in Jerusalem come from Bethlehem, where the industry has been established since the end of the Middle Ages. The population of Bethlehem includes a number of peo-

BETHLEHEM. The Altar of the Nativity, in the Grotto of the Basilica of the Nativity. Courtesy, Levant Photo Service

BETHLEHEM. Church of the Nativity. Entrance shows three doors, the two older ones filled in.

ple with fair skin and hair, probably descended from the Crusaders.

Beyond the ancient reservoirs of Solomon's Pools there are a
number of villages which are engaged in agriculture, and neat
rows of vines and other trees and crops can be seen at the side
of the road. The grapes from here are made into wine for
export. Some of the villages are quite large, such as Halhuf, but
the center for this part of the Hill Country is Hebron, one of the
oldest cities in the world and a place hallowed in Jewish, Christian and Moslem tradition. It has never grown to a large size
but has persisted throughout the centuries as a market town
serving the local villages. It is also a pilgrimage center, especially
for Jews who now flock there in great numbers. Under Jordanian administration, the town was very dependent on Jerusalem for its tourists, since it had no hotels, but now with access
possible from all sides, this tie is weakening. Hebron has industries of some importance, especially in glassware and metal-
ware, and much of the produce is sent to the souvenir shops in
Jerusalem.

South of Hebron, the rainfall decreases considerably and so
do the villages, and the hills decline in elevation as the Negev is
reached. This region of semi-desert has generally remained un-
settled, although there was a flourishing civilization here in
Byzantine times, which no doubt had strong ties with the city
of Jerusalem. Throughout most of its history, however, the Negev
has been the home of tribes of nomads.

THE WESTERN AXIS

West of Jerusalem there has always been an axis of inter-
relationship with the coastal towns and the international highway running along the eastern part of the coastal plain. In
this direction Jerusalem has maintained its links with the Mediterranean, and it has been along this line that most pilgrims
have approached the city. It is also to the west that the city has
spread most outside the old walls, beginning in the latter half of
the nineteenth century. This axis and the routes which followed
it assumed considerable importance between 1948 and 1967 in
linking Western Jerusalem with the rest of Israel.

There are three main routeways which follow this axis, the
actual routes and their significance varying from age to age.
The "natural" approach to Jerusalem would appear to be the valley of the Soreq, leading up from the area of Beth Shemesh.
However, because of its steep and winding nature it has often

been more of an impediment to movement than an aid. Although used by a railway it is not followed by any major road. The three routeways are:

(1) A northern route which leaves Jerusalem via the northern branch of the upper Soreq and crosses the river near the village of Qaluniya. This stretch of country just to the west of the new Jerusalem is undulating and well wooded and is planned to be a green belt under the Israel Master Plan. The route then traverses a ridge of higher land and descends the upper part of the Wadi Kabir to Latrun and Imwas (the favorite candidate for the site of ancient Emmaus). These were popular stops on the route to Jerusalem but have suffered from twenty years of being on the hottest armistice line in the post-war era. The route continues on to Ramleh, the old Moslem capital of Palestine and built in the eighth century A.D. by the Omayyads to replace Lydda (Lod) as the administrative seat. Both Ramleh and Lydda are surrounded by orchards, although they are in rapid danger of becoming outer suburbs of Tel Aviv. Certainly their contacts with Jerusalem have not been strong, except when pilgrimages were in full swing.

(2) The second routeway to the west goes to Ein Karem, now an outer suburb of Jewish Jerusalem, and from there crosses the northern branch of the Soreq and follows a ridge to the village of Ishwa from which one road leads to Beth Shemesh and another takes the new road to Ramleh. Beth Shemesh, although an old site and one of the northern border towns of Judah (Josh. 15:10), was only an ancient mound until Israeli planners transformed it into a new urban center with a large sugar factory and other industries. It thus acts as a center for the western end of the Jerusalem corridor and has strong relations with the capital. This central routeway continues across the coastal plain to Ashdod on the coast.

(3) A third routeway leaves Jerusalem south of Ein Karem and crosses the Soreq (here called the Refaim) south of 'Aqqur. Then the route continues practically parallel with the old armistice line to Beit Guvrin, which is on the site of a large Byzantine town called Eleutheropolis. In ancient times this routeway provided a link with several important towns in the southern part of the Shephelah and the coastal plain, such as Lachish, Ashqelon and Gaza. It is now less used and the roads are not good.

The Axis to the East

The links between Jerusalem and the settlements to the east have been strongly influenced by two physical barriers, the Wilderness of Judea, which separated the city from the Jericho and Qumran oasis, and the Jordan River, which separates the whole of Western Palestine from the scarp and plateau of Transjordan.

To the immediate east of Jerusalem lies the Mount of Olives and a little group of ancient villages, such as Bethany and et-Tur and Abu Dis. These villages, with a strong interest in the tourist trade, have always maintained the strongest links with Jerusalem and can almost be classed as suburbs of the city. Beyond them is the arid wilderness and this has helped to thrust them even closer to Jerusalem. Apart from the tourist industry and a growing commuter population, these villages are largely agricultural, including some dairying.

Beyond the wilderness is the oasis of Jericho which acts as a link between the Jerusalem region and Transjordan. The climate has made Jericho a popular winter resort from ancient times onwards. The Roman irrigation channels, like those of today, produced a large amount of fruit and vegetables for the Jerusalem hotels and hospices. Is it little wonder that Zacchaeus was wealthy with this kind of tax district (Luke 19)!

Beyond the Jordan there are a large number of towns and villages which in ancient times prospered from a large agricultural production and trade with the desert tribes. However, the links with Jerusalem have not always been strong, although from 1948 to 1967 there were strong commercial and administrative links between Jerusalem and Amman.

We can see that it is not easy to define a region for Jerusalem, such as is possible for many cities in Europe and North America. Often the city has been overshadowed by larger ones and has been relegated to the role of a small pilgrimage center. At other times it has been a large city and the center for most of Palestine. In many respects it has played a dual role, as a world center from the religious point of view, but in the strict commercial sense only serving the central Hill Country. Hence it has preserved its unique character and has been comparatively unspoiled by industrial growth. It acts as a market town to the surrounding towns and villages from the Shiloh area to the northern Negev. Its immediate region is small; yet its main economic activity, the pilgrim-tourist industry, gives it a region which today extends to the beaches of California in the West and the islands of Japan in the East.

II

THE SITE – RELIEF AND CLIMATE

As the mountains are round about Jerusalem,
So the Lord is round about his people. – Psalm 125:2

The crest of the Judean hills marks the dividing line between the drainage basin of the Mediterranean and that of the Dead Sea, and just east of this crest lies Jerusalem. The city stands on a promontory or headland, formed by two valleys which unite just south of this headland and run towards the Dead Sea. The promontory itself is split into two unequal ridges by a smaller valley, called (to use Josephus' term) the Tyropoeon Valley. Beyond the eastern of the two large valleys, the Kidron, lies the Mount of Olives and its extension to the north, Mount Scopus. Beyond the western valley, the Hinnom, lies the Western Hill which forms part of the high crest of the Hill Country. To the south of Jerusalem lie the Mount of Offence, really a southern extension of the Mount of Olives, and the Hill of Evil Counsel. These hills, beyond the bounds of ancient Jerusalem are all higher than the promontory on which the city stands and hide any distant views except to the southeast where the hills of Transjordan can be seen through the gap between the Mount of Offence and the Hill of Evil Counsel.

It is important in any study of the site of Jerusalem to remember that the present Old City and the hills immediately south of it do not rest on natural rock but rather on centuries of rubble and ruins which have practically obliterated that important feature of the original site, the Tyropoeon Valley. The difference in profile between the present contours of the surface relief and the natural rock contours, first mapped by Charles Warren,[1]

---

1 Sir C. Warren and C. R. Conder, *The Survey of Western Palestine: Jerusalem* (1884).

28

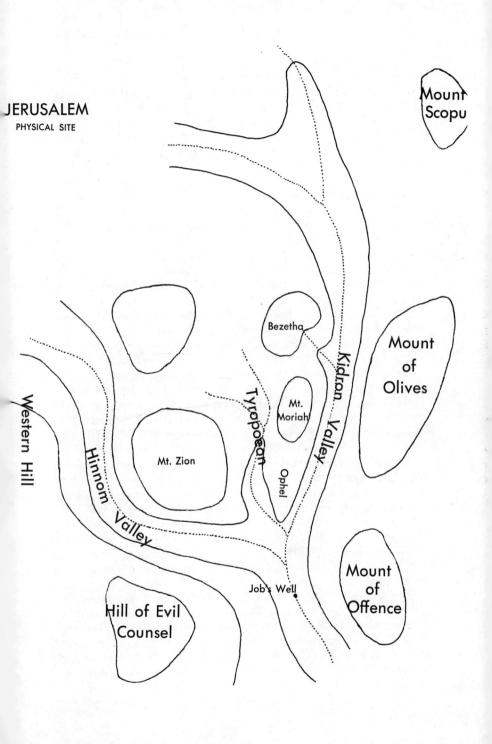

JERUSALEM
PHYSICAL SITE

Mount Scopu

Mount of Olives

Mount of Offence

Bezetha

Mt. Moriah

Ophel

Mt. Zion

Kidron Valley

Tyropoeon

Western Hill

Hinnom Valley

Hill of Evil Counsel

Job's Well

can be seen on page 29. Thus the contrast between the low elevation of the city and the height of the surrounding hills must have
been considerably greater in ancient times, when the city was
up to ninety feet lower than at present. As the surrounding
hills have only recently been built on, they have little depth
of superficial deposits, and so the general effect of 3,000 years
or so of human occupation has been to raise the promontory
in relation to the surrounding hills.

However, it is the native rock which influenced the occupation
of the original site and a knowledge of the geological back-
ground of Jerusalem is very important to an understanding of
its subsequent development. The character of the rock and the
alignment of the strata, or layers of rock, determine many
things — the water supply, the soils, the building material and
even the location of graveyards. The nature of the solid rock
under Jerusalem is not known too exactly. Max Blanckenhorn,
who produced the first accurate map of the geology of the city,
was forced simply to classify much of the area as building debris.[2] Basically, however, we can now recognize three north-
south strands of surface rock. These strands represent the exposed parts of three layers of material of different age. These
rocks were then arched up to form what geologists call an anticline, which was the beginning of the Judean Hill Country.
Jerusalem is situated on what is the eastern flank of that anticline, with the rock strata dipping in an easterly direction. The
subsequent erosion of the top of the anticline, has thus left the
three layers of rock side by side in parallel north-south lines.

The oldest of these rocks and the westernmost strand, is called
the *Cenomanian*. It is hard — too hard for the tombs of all but
the richest — but weathers to a good soil and forms a large
block west of the Hinnom and under the new Jewish city.
The old builders called this rock *mizzi ahmar* and *mizzi yahudi*.
It gives a high quality of hard building stone, but is difficult
(and therefore expensive) to quarry, as it consists largely of
limestone and dolomite, the oldest of the rocks in the Jerusalem area.

The strand of rock exposed east of the Cenomanian is
called the *Turonian* and is the basic material of the promontory on which the Old City stands between the Hinnom and the
Kidron. It has many similarities to the Cenomanian and in some
places, such as the Negev, geologists have had difficulty in
distinguishing between the two. It consists of two layers, the

2 M. Blanckenhorn, *Z.D.P.V.* (1905).

lower of which is called *meleke* and was classified by some early geologists in the Cenomanian. It is softer than the latter, however, but hardens on exposure and has thus been popular as a building stone, especially for public buildings. It can be seen in Solomon's Quarries in the northern part of the Old City. The other Turonian band is known as the *mizzi helu*, and is not as soft as the meleke, but occurs in thin layers and so is easy to work. Apart from being good for building purposes, the Turonian rock also is rich in flints, weathers to a good soil and can be easily dug for tombs. Consequently, it was the one with all the advantages for the early inhabitants of the area.

The *Senonian* chalks are the third strand of surface rock and are dominant under the Mount of Olives and the hills to the south of Jerusalem. This white, soft rock has a fireproof quality but is otherwise not as useful as the other two layers. It is too soft for building purposes and even tombs dug into it tend to collapse, while it forms a poor soil and gets slippery when wet.

It can be seen, then, that the valleys of the Kidron and the Hinnom form not only boundaries of relief features but of the bedrock as well. It seems that there are zones of weakness along the joints between the major strata which have been followed by the storm torrents which eroded out the two valleys.[3] The fact that the settlers of this area have always built on the Turonian promontory except when economic conditions have forced them further out, has not happened by chance but is in large measure a result of the geomorphological characteristics which we have seen. The steep valleys on either side of the promontory, eroded away by centuries of storm brooks, gave the early settlers good defenses; the abundance of flints and the good soil on the Turonian encouraged them to settle; the presence of excellent building stone in and around their early encampments made it easy for them to build their houses, palaces and temples.

It is worth noting that all the rocks mentioned are limestones, characterized by their ability to absorb water and to dissolve into cave formation. The only other surface deposits in the area are the Quaternary materials, especially on the top of the Mount of Olives, which consists mainly of clays, soil and sub-soil. A geological influence not mentioned so far is that of the earthquakes, which from time to time have shaken the Mediterranean lands. Their occurrence in Jerusalem is frequent, but

---

3 M. Avniemelech, *B.A.S.O.R.* (February, 1966).

they have not reached the ferocity of those in the Jordan rift valley. They have been blamed for stopping springs in the city and have shaken houses from time to time, but have had no drastic effects.

THE OPHEL-MORIAH RIDGE

The promontory of Turonian rock is not a simple feature and must be dealt with in more detail in order to understand the site of Jerusalem. The promontory, as mentioned above, consists of two ridges separated by the Tyropoeon valley. The eastern ridge is very narrow — especially in its natural rock state — and many early scholars on account of this, were reluctant to accept this as the site of David's city. The basic rock of the ridge is the Turonian limestone, but it is ringed by Quaternary river deposits in the two valleys which flank it. The ridge can be divided into three parts:

(1) The southern spur — generally referred to as Ophel.
(2) The broader hill on which the Haram esh Sharif and formerly the Temple were built. This hill is often called Mt. Moriah.
(3) The Bezetha Hill, the hill to the north of the Haram, in what is now known as the Moslem Quarter.

The Ophel spur rises gradually from its tip, just southeast of the Pool of Siloam at 2100 feet above sea level (Mediterranean datum) to 2297 feet on the shoulder between the Dung Gate and the Virgin's Fountain. As has been pointed out, the original hill seems to have been smaller and steeper than at present and there seems to have been deliberate terracing by early rulers of the city to broaden the ridge. Some scholars consider this to be the origin of the term "Millo," i.e. filling, mentioned in connection with David's building in the city (II Sam. 5:9) and elsewhere. The shoulder between the present Dung Gate and the Virgin's Fountain, where the ascent of the ridge is checked, has been the subject of some controversy, as many scholars consider that the hill on which the Acra fortress of Hasmonaean times (and possibly also the Zion fortress of David) was here. The contours, however, both rock and surface, seem perfectly natural at this point and there is no hint of the drastic change in the relief which the Hasmonaean destruction of the Acra hill would have brought about. The steep sides of the Ophel ridge were a considerable aid in the defense of the

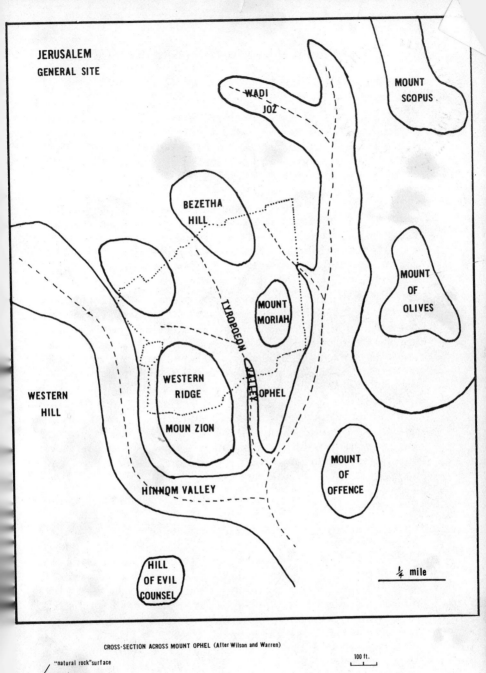

JERUSALEM
GENERAL SITE

WADI JOZ

MOUNT SCOPUS

BEZETHA HILL

MOUNT OF OLIVES

TYROPOEON VALLEY

MOUNT MORIAH

OPHEL

WESTERN HILL

WESTERN RIDGE

MOUN ZION

HINNOM VALLEY

MOUNT OF OFFENCE

HILL OF EVIL COUNSEL

¼ mile

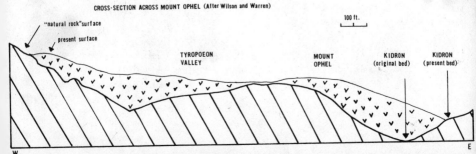

CROSS-SECTION ACROSS MOUNT OPHEL (After Wilson and Warren)

100 ft.

"natural rock" surface
present surface

TYROPOEON VALLEY

MOUNT OPHEL

KIDRON (original bed)

KIDRON (present bed)

W   E

early city, however, and the proximity of the Virgin's Fountain spring made this site attractive.

Mount Moriah is very largely flattened out by the Haram enclosure, and without going into the underground caverns, one can only see it in its "natural" state in the Sakhra rock. This hill is 2430 feet above sea level on the platform of the Dome of the Rock, thus representing a rise of 100 meters from the tip of Ophel, with a gradient on the average of about 1 in 8, not too steep for settlement by Oriental standards. In the Sakhra rock, the limestone appears as a rocky knoll with a cave underneath, in part natural, but probably enlarged by man. The eastern ridge is much broader at this point, so the Haram enclosure provides peaceful gardens in the middle of a busy city and probably is one of the oldest urban parks in existence.

North of the Moriah hill was a ravine under what is now St. Anne's Church, since filled in with rubble. A ditch was hewn out north of the Haram. Beyond this ditch and between the upper Tyropoeon and the St. Anne ravine, is a hill aligned in a northwest to southeast direction and composed on the surface of the *mizzi helu* limestone and rising to 2540 feet near the so-called "Solomon's Quarries." This hill seems to have been the Bezetha hill of Josephus (Wars, 5:4). It was not incorporated into the walled city until the first century A.D., when it was a fashionable suburb. The quarries known as Solomon's Quarries are in the northwestern part of this hill, where the meleke rock underneath the *mizzi helu* is exposed and was quarried for building stone.

THE WESTERN RIDGE (MT. ZION)

The western ridge of the Jerusalem promontory, between the Hinnom and the Tyropoeon, is much broader than the Ophel-Moriah ridge. In its natural state it presented a much more gentle and roomier aspect, making it popular as a fashionable residential area and a place for gardens and cemeteries. In Biblical times it was the "upper city" and main civilian suburb; in Arab and Ottoman times it was covered with burial sites, gardens and churches. In view of its elevated nature (2550 ft.) it was popular with the upper classes, as they were out of range of the smells and squalor of the less wealthy citizens (as long as the wind was a westerly!), and there are remains of first-century streets and houses, including two large residences attributed to the high priest Caiaphas. Today, outside the city walls and covered gardens, the southern part of the ridge is still

ST. ANNE'S CHURCH, of Crusader origin. Shows damage incurred during the 1967 war.

known popularly as Mt. Zion, but the presence of the 1948 armistice line has limited its use. Inside the present walls, the ridge continues in the area of the Armenian Quarter, also with large gardens.

The discovery of the real rock contours revealed a branch of the Tyropoeon valley not known before, running between David Street and the Holy Sepulcher Church, thus dividing the western ridge into two parts. The hill north of this valley is really a continuation of the ridge on which the old Russian colony stands and it reaches 2600 feet in height in the area of the Qasr Jalud, at the northwest angle of the city walls. The slopes here are gentle and there is a spur to the southeast under the present Holy Sepulcher Church. This higher western ridge has been occupied by the Christian and Armenian communities, these being generally richer than the Moslems because of their interest in trade and commerce, and so again, the wealthier citizens have chosen the higher land above the smells of the lower quarters.

HILL OF EVIL COUNSEL

The Hill of Evil Counsel, or to give it its native name, Jebel Abu Tor, lies south of the Hinnom valley where it swings eastward around Mt. Zion. Formed largely of Senonian chalk, it rises to 2560 feet, but as the chalk gives little encouragement to settlement and the hill has no water supply, it has only been built on extensively in recent decades. Its northern slopes have provided burial grounds for Jerusalem and it has in the past had a defensive function of guarding the approach to Jerusalem from the south, the old Hebron road passing on its western slopes. It appears but rarely in the records of the city, however, but the origin of its name (from the tradition that here Caiaphas took counsel on what to do with Jesus), suggests that it might have been used as a retreat or quiet place out of the city.

THE WESTERN HILL

To the west of the Hinnom valley is a series of hills carved out of the Cenomanian limestone which represent the crest of the Hill Country and the water-parting between the Mediterranean and the drainage basin of the Jordan. Rising up to nearly 2650 feet above sea level, this hill hides Jerusalem from the west and several travelers have noted the suddenness of the appearance of the Old City when arriving from this direction. The harder

Cenomanian limestone, less useful than the Turonian, did not encourage settlement to the west, especially as there were no good defensive sites in this area. However, in the nineteenth century, with the onset of pilgrimages from the wealthier classes in Western Europe and the Zionist immigrations into Palestine, buildings began to spring up outside the northwest corner of the city walls and later to the south, after a railway station had been built. Now most of the city is built over these western hills.

THE MOUNT OF OLIVES

Perhaps the most famous of all the hills surrounding the Old City of Jerusalem, is the one to the east, the Mount of Olives. The hill is largely carved out of Senonian chalk with a band of *mizzi helu* on the lower part of the western slopes and Quaternary deposits on the surface east of the summit. As it rises to over 2600 feet, the view from the summit is justly praised, giving an excellent view to the east and also over the Old City itself. Like the Western Hill, however, it has only been built over in recent decades and in fact most of the present houses are of post-1948 date. This is partly because of the rock surface, as pointed out above, but also the distance from the city. In addition, the rainfall decreases notably at this point and east of the hill only two villages are found before the wilderness sets in. Although the soil is not good, a small dairy farm has been functioning near the summit in recent years and this may prove a good way of improving the soil by adding organic matter. The Mount of Olives is, however, an asset principally because of its tourist interest. It has many New Testament associations and magnificent views, and it is essential that it should not be too highly developed.

South of the main road to Jericho and east of the village of Silwan, is the Mount of Offence (Jebel batn el-Hawa), formed like the Mount of Olives, of which it is a continuation, of Senonian chalk on a Turonian base. Apart from its western slopes it has never been built on because of poor soils and distance from the city. Another continuation of the Mount of Olives, this time to the north, is Mount Scopus which guards the approach to Jerusalem from the north. Its fine prospect of the city was utilized in A.D. 70 by the Roman armies in their siege of Jerusalem and the hill also held a Jewish enclave in Jordanian territory from 1948 to 1967.

The Northern Plateau

Mention should be made of the plateau to the north of the Old City, bounded on the east by the upper Kidron (Wadi Joz). This plateau is a comparatively level tract of land with only small hillocks, notably that known as Gordon's Calvary, breaking out of the plain. Although not built upon until the end of the last century (apart from a brief expansion in the Byzantine era), this part of the environs of Jerusalem has been of importance because it is the obvious approach for any enemy wishing to attack the city. Jerusalem is well defended on all sides except the north, so most attacks have come from this direction. Because of the constant need to build strong walls on this side of the city and the high quality of the Turonian and Cenomanian outcrops to the north, several old quarries are found here, such as Jeremiah's Grotto. An extensive Moslem cemetery, as well as remains of ancient burials, are also found here.

The Kidron Valley

Of the valleys in the Jerusalem area, the Kidron is probably the most important. It does not hold a permanent stream and its bed is now so choked that only a small trickle flows down it except after heavy rain. In former times it may have been more significant, for there are ample references to the "brook" Kidron (e.g. II Chron. 23:12; John 18:1). It is clear, however, that the watercourse was a storm stream only and never a large obstacle and it was the valley rather than the brook which was of significance to Josephus (Wars, 5:2). Judging from Solomon's warning to Shimei (I Kings 2:37), the water does seem to have acted as a city boundary. Much of the deposit on the valley floor is of geologically recent date and there is fifty feet or more difference between the present bed and the rock underneath, although lower down, past Silwan, the bed is natural rock.

The river deposits in the valley, together with the fact that water is more abundant here than on the hills, has given rise to cultivation below the city walls, and the valley has become a favorite spot for gardens. In the lands of the fringe of the arid zone, it is difficult to cultivate gardens on the hill slopes, as rainfall runs down the slope so quickly and often takes the soil with it; so the tree cultivation tends to be limited to the hardy and strong rooted varieties such as the olive, fig and vine. In valleys such as the Kidron, there is an accumulation of moisture and of soil, ideal conditions for intensive cultivation. Hence there are frequent references to gardens in the Kidron in the

KIDRON VALLEY. View southeast from the Old City wall, Jerusalem. The village of Silwan is visible at the left. Courtesy, Levant Photo Service

KIDRON VALLEY. View northeast from the Old City wall, Jerusalem. Visible are the Garden of Gethsemane, Church of All Nations, Russian Church, and the Mount of Olives.

Bible and in later literature also. The lush vegetation of the present Garden of Gethsemane stands in marked contrast to the general level of cultivation on the Mount of Olives, and the valley seems to have acted as a "green belt" preventing urban development to the east.

A brief mention here might be made of the spring known as the Virgin's Fountain, which originally issued forth into the Kidron valley east of the Ophel ridge, but was diverted in ancient times to flow via a tunnel into the Tyropoeon. This spring probably originally made the lower part of the Kidron valley a permanent stream until the water eventually seeped into the thirsty ground. This spring was a very important source of water to the ancient city, and will be dealt with in more detail in the next chapter.

HINNOM VALLEY

This valley, known in Arabic as the Wadi er-Rababi, has its origin in the Western Hill in the new suburbs of the Jewish city. Its stream "flows" eastward, receiving a left bank tributary at the Pool of Mamilla, where it slowly bends towards the south and, following the zone between the Cenomanian and Turonian rock beds, curves round the Old City to join the Kidron below the village of Silwan and just north of Job's Well. The valley has suffered somewhat in tradition compared with the Kidron and has been looked on as evil. The atrocities of some of the kings of Biblical times, such as Ahaz (II Chron. 28:3), have given it a bad name and it was in this valley that the city's rubbish was burned, giving the continual flames which lent their name to the Gehenna of Jesus. It has held two pools, and aqueducts flowed across it; but the valley has never had the pleasant green atmosphere of the Kidron. Instead it has been used as a Moslem cemetery and has been the scene of a cattle market and refuse dumps. Nevertheless, the Hinnom has provided a valuable defensive line for the Old City on its western side and although generally dry, has been used for gardens in its lower reaches. In addition, its rather more gentle slopes compared with the Kidron, have enabled it to be used for building purposes.

TYROPOEON VALLEY

The third valley of Jerusalem is not given a name in the Bible, but Josephus refers to it as the Tyropoeon valley, or the valley of the Cheesemakers, and to the present local inhabitants it is known simply as El Wad. It divides the western and eastern ridges of the Jerusalem promontory and originally must have been quite an impressive feature. The accumulation of rubble in this valley, and the constant building in and over it, has raised its level so much that its course is no longer obvious, and it is difficult to discern in places where it was once of vital importance. Consequently it is in the case of the Tyropoeon valley that the contrast between the present and the rock surfaces is seen most clearly. The valley has its origin north of the Damascus Gate, where it lies equidistant between the line of the Kidron and that of the Hinnom. It then runs (one cannot say "flows" as there has yet been found no proof that it ever carried a stream of any degree of permanence) in a south-easterly direction until it approaches the Haram walls, which are built over the eastern bank of this valley. Then it runs south, being joined by a right-bank tributary, now largely obscured, from the Muristan area, and continues under the present Dung Gate to join the Kidron just before its junction with the Hinnom.

The Tyropoeon has been of considerable importance to Jerusalem in the past, more so than at the present time. It provided a defense to the west for the early city of Ophel and in later times acted as the main drain (to the detriment of the Virgin's Fountain!) as well as a site for gardens in post-Jewish times. Remains of viaducts linking the western and eastern ridges across this valley are visible in Robinson's and Wilson's Arches. Although the valley is now built over in its upper part and was once also inhabited in its lower reaches, it has essentially acted in times past as a divide between the "upper" and the "lower" city and was probably as much a social as a physical barrier. Although never carrying a surface stream, there were pools in its lower reaches, one of which, the Pool of Siloam, being fed by tunnel from the Virgin's Fountain.

Mention has already been made of Jerusalem's location on the margin of the arid zone, sufficient perhaps to indicate that climate plays an important role in the geography of the city. It is not enough to assume that the weather received by the inhabitants of Jerusalem is generally the same as that in the rest of Palestine and of no significance in detail. Local variations in climate have been very important in determining water supply and urban growth.

Palestine is climatically shared by two zones: the Mediter-

ranean and the Arid Zones.[4] The greater area is under the
Mediterranean regime, with its hot, dry summers and mild but
wet winters, but certain areas such as the Jordan valley and the
southern half of the Negev are within the arid zone, with its
hot temperatures and low, erratic rainfall. There is a considerable belt of country which is marginal to these two zones, the
northern part of the Negev and the Wilderness of Judea. The
characteristic of the arid zone which is best known is its low
rainfall, but it is not just lack of rain which is the main problem,
but its unreliability, most marked at the margins.[5] Palestine has
so often been a battleground between the desert and the moister
Mediterranean zone, and the unreliability of rainfall in the belt
between the two has been of considerable geographical significance.

Jerusalem is situated just east of the crest of the Hill Country
and here a rain shadow effect begins to operate. Clouds coming
in from the west have often been seen to disappear as they approach the Mount of Olives, having deposited rain over the
Western Hill, and many observers have noted that there may
be an apparently permanent dark cloud over the Jewish city
while the sky above the Mount of Olives is clear. This explains
the concern of many of Jerusalem's rulers for the water supply,
for while in a good year cisterns are adequate, in a dry spell
they are insufficient and many times at the end of summer following a dry winter, Job's Well has been the only source of water
for the citizens. Fortunately the weather records for Jerusalem
are long compared with most cities in the Middle East, thanks
to the work of Glaisher, Chaplin and MacGowan.[6] These figures
all show this great variation in rainfall from year to year, which
we shall now examine.[7]

RAINFALL

The rainfall in Palestine is largely concentrated in the winter
months with a peak about December-February, when the country lies in the belt of westerly depressions bringing in moist air
from the Mediterranean Sea. More rain falls in the hills than
on the coastal plain, but east of the crest of the Hill Country

---

4 Orni and Efrat, *Geography of Israel*, p. 105 ff.

5 For the problems of the Arid Zone, see E. S. Hills, *Arid Lands: A Geographical Appraisal* (1966).

6 For the meteorological reports of these early observers, see the *Quarterly
Statements* of the Palestine Exploration Fund.

7 For analysis of figures, see N. Rosenau, *I.E.J.* (1955).

the air descends to the Jordan valley and having deposited most of its moisture has little to give to the wilderness area. In Jerusalem, there is no month when rain cannot occur, for even in summer, convection storms can bring relief from the heat and sun. There is a tendency toward rather larger falls of rain at the beginning and end of the rainy season, corresponding to the "former" and "latter" rains of the Bible. In 1965, for example, there was a long dry period in January and February, but March was cold and wet. These later showers can be of vital importance to the farmer.

The rain shadow effect has already been mentioned and it is significant that the amount of settlement and agriculture east of Jerusalem is considerably less than that to the west. The rainfall shows a distinct falling off as one goes east, and the western suburbs of Jewish Jerusalem receive considerably more moisture than the villages on the eastern slopes of the Mount of Olives. The variation in district is accompanied by variability in time. The important "latter rain that watereth the earth" (Hosea 6:3) occurred, for example, in 1962, with an April total much larger than that for March; but in 1963, there was a steady decline after a February peak of 4.7 inches. The annual total can also vary. Up to 1955, the average since readings first began was 21.8 inches (about the same as the eastern counties of England), but the total has been as high as 42.5 inches and as low as 8.1 inches. So Jerusalem never quite reaches the desert rainfall totals of less than 8 inches, but there is obviously considerable uncertainty as to how much will fall in any one year and also when and where it will fall.

Snow is not very frequent in the city and although the statistical average is two days of snowfall a year, in practice Jerusalem usually gets a week or so of snow every five to ten years. Dew can occur and is important as a supplementary source of moisture, but is not as frequent as near the coast, for humidity on the hills is relatively low.

TEMPERATURE

The temperature regime in Jerusalem also shows some variation both month to month and between day and night. It is more variable than on the coast, where the sea exerts a moderating influence, but less extreme than on the plateau of Transjordan. In general the temperatures are cooler than on the coast, because of the height of the Hill Country, and so the area has often been used as a summer resort for inhabitants of lower altitudes.

The range of temperature throughout the year and also the diurnal range are greater in Jerusalem than in Tel Aviv or Haifa. From year to year there can be variations in winter temperature, but during the summer the heat which the inhabitants endure is much the same each year. Winters do show some variation, however, and often January can be quite fine and warm while April is cool and wet. There is little or no areal variation in temperature over the city, although the hills tend to be cooler and more pleasant than the valleys in summer as they catch the breezes. Winds, in fact, play an important part in the city's weather, and usually exert a pleasant cooling influence. Sometimes, however, the city experiences a dry "Sirocco" wind from the eastern desert, once described by one of the city's prophets as "a hot wind from the bare heights in the wilderness toward the daughter of my people, not to fan nor to cleanse" (Jer. 4: 11). This hot, dry wind can cause considerable discomfort.

The general characteristics of the climate of Jerusalem are, however, its unreliability of rainfall and its coolness of temperature compared with the coast and the desert. The latter characteristic has helped to make the city an attractive resort for those Palestinians living in the hotter and more humid parts; but the rainfall unreliability has caused considerable headaches to the citizens, and the many pools and aqueducts bear testimony to Jerusalem's attempts to make itself independent of rain as the source of water.

III

WATER SUPPLY

There is a river, the streams whereof shall make glad the
city of God, the holy place of the tabernacles of the Most
High. — Psalm 46:4

We have already seen that Jerusalem is situated just east of
the water-parting of the Hill Country and on the verge of the
arid wilderness. It is not surprising therefore to learn that
with a rainfall which is both unreliable and not very well dis-
tributed, the supply of water has always been a problem to
the citizens. Frequent years of drought have dried up the cisterns and made obtaining water a difficult and arduous task.
This condition is typical of settlements on the fringe of the arid
zone, for while within the deserts proper the only reliable source
of water is underground wells or springs, on the fringe it is often
tempting to rely on rainfall.[1] In many places springs are fed
by rainfall, permeating into the layers of rock underground, or
in some favored areas there might be an "exotic" river which
receives its supplies from moister areas, as is the case with the
Nile. Other sources of supply in dry climates are wells sunk into
water-bearing strata. At the present time progress is being
made toward the conversion of sea water for domestic and industrial use.

For Jerusalem, the nature of the site limits the water supply
to two possible sources: rainfall and ground water, as there are
no perennial streams flowing near the city. As physical controls, the sources of water have been very important in influencing the morphological development of Jerusalem, and in
ancient times the city clung tenaciously to the spring and tun-

---

1 See Hills, *Arid Lands.*

nel by the Ophel hill. It was only as outside sources became available and greater efficiency was achieved in the utilization of rainwater, that the city was enabled to expand away from its natural sources of the precious liquid.

The ultimate source of all water is rainfall, but generally only a proportion of the water which falls on the surface of the ground eventually forms surface streams, as a large amount sinks into the ground and some evaporates off into the atmosphere. In the case of limestone country, the percentage of water absorbed is very high and surface streams are generally lacking, but there may be considerable activity underground. It is on underground sources that Jerusalem relies for its basic supply, either from the immediate vicinity or sources further away.

It might be recalled that the Hinnom Valley lies at the junction between the hard Cenomanian limestone, which is relatively impervious (although no limestone is completely impervious) and the Turonian. While the Cenomanian would be likely to carry some surface water, there is considerable sinkage into the Turonian and the valley rarely carries a running stream. It is in the Kidron Valley, in fact, that most hydrological activity is found, for here we get the most active stream in the district and also the one true spring in Jerusalem. The Kidron stream is not perennial, however, but a storm brook (*nahal*) and flows in winter after heavy rain but dries up in summer. It receives much effluent and can be very unpleasant. There is an ancient well below the junction of the Kidron and the Hinnom, called Bir Eiyub or Job's Well, which is used by those villagers in the vicinity; but it is too far from the city to be of much use today, and even in ancient times was probably used only as a reserve supply. So the main source of water for the ancient city was the spring of the Virgin's Fountain on the side of the Ophel ridge and this was supplemented in Roman times by an aqueduct bringing water from outside, from the so-called Solomon's Pools. Today the water for the city is all piped from outside sources.

It must not be forgotten that much of the city's supply has always been directly from rainwater collected in cisterns and this has been the usual system of obtaining water in the winter months in all the villages and towns of Palestine. In a wet year such a supply can sometimes last the whole year round, but usually it has to be supplemented by spring or well water; hence the presence of these underground sources of supply has been a strong factor controlling settlement location in this area since earliest times.

We shall now have a look at the sources of Jerusalem's supply in more detail and see the influence of this physical control on the morphology of the city.

THE VIRGIN'S FOUNTAIN (EN SITTI MARIAM)

The only natural spring in Jerusalem, as mentioned above, is that known as En Sitti Mariam or the Virgin's Fountain. Another Arab name for it is 'En Umm ed-Derej, which means Fountain of the Steps. There are hints in the Bible and elsewhere of other springs in Jerusalem, but this is the only one known today and the stratification of the rocks underlying the city would suggest that this is the only likely place anyway. It lies at the foot of the hill of Ophel, below the eastern scarp and opposite the northern end of the village of Silwan, thus being about half way between the Temple enclosure and the tip of Ophel. This location makes it accessible, although not very easily defensible, as a source of water for any settlement on the summit of Ophel. At the present time it serves as the main water supply for the village of Silwan as well as being a considerable tourist attraction.

As has been mentioned above, the spring emerges here because the Turonian limestone in which the rainwater is absorbed is exposed by the Kidron and reduced to such a narrow depth below surface that water emerges and flows onto the surface. Although the spring is now reached by steps leading down into a small pool, it originally issued forth and flowed down the Kidron, eventually seeping underground. The deposition of water-borne material onto the valley floor, as well as the human debris accumulated in this area, has had the effect of raising the valley floor and so the spring now no longer issues onto the surface.

There are several interesting passages and fissures around the spring, two being aqueducts which will receive greater attention later. There is also a shaft which leads from the level of the spring upwards to a horizontal passage, which, via a flight of steps, emerges onto the surface of Ophel. This interesting system is known as Warren's Shaft (after its discoverer) and is considered to be the old method by which the inhabitants on Ophel reached the spring, especially in times of seige when the normal approach was impossible. This system may well be the "watercourse" of II Samuel 5:8, by which David gained entry to Jebus.

One interesting feature of the Virgin's Fountain is its famous turbulence. The spring has a very uneven flow, gushing forth from two to five times each day (less in summer and more in winter), between periods of low-level quiescence. The native inhabitants explain this by reference to a legend of a dragon who, when awake, drinks the water, but when asleep lets it all flow past. The real reason for this phenomenon is probably that the reservoir of water in the Turonian layers under Jerusalem, fed by rain waters, seeps slowly down and builds up in a natural syphon behind a fissure less than one foot wide, which was examined by Conrad Schick during an exceptionally dry period. On reaching a certain level it gushes out. The ultimate source of the water being rainfall, the flow naturally is greater in winter than in summer, but the system has yet to be thoroughly examined by a hydrologist.

Now, how does this spring fit in with the various names of water sources mentioned in the Bible? In the Scriptures we read of many springs and pools — Gihon, En Rogel, Bethesda, Siloam, etc. Most scholars now accept that the Virgin's Fountain is the old spring of Gihon, where Solomon was anointed and proclaimed king (I Kings 1:38-40). In fact there are only two springs mentioned as such in the Bible, i.e. Gihon and En Rogel, other sources being really pools or aqueducts. Another name which occurs is the "Dragon Well" of Nehemiah 2:13. If the name En Rogel is taken at its face value, i.e. Fullers' Spring, it can only refer to the Virgin's Fountain, as the other candidate, Bir Eiyub, is a well. However, the term for spring in Arabic ('Ain) is used very loosely, as in the case of 'Ain Silwan; so little reliance can be placed on it. In the anointing of Solomon it is recorded that he went "down" to Gihon, and then "came up" to Jerusalem afterwards, a description which would fit in well with the Virgin's Fountain. Manasseh built a wall around Gihon (II Chron. 33:14) which could not have been Bir Eiyub, as it is too far away. The final witness, however, is the existence of Hezekiah's tunnel. The chronicler records that Hezekiah "stopped the upper water-course of Gihon and brought it straight down to the west side of the city of David" and the tunnel by which this was done is now visible for all who care to explore it. This identification of Gihon with the Virgin's Fountain does not, of course, rule out the possibility of other names being applied to it, such as that of the "Dragon Well," but it does rule out the view held by many nineteenth century scholars that Gihon was to the west of the present Old City in the area of the Birket Mamilla. In any case, from what we now know of the location of the original Zion, the older theory is highly un-likely.

JOB'S WELL (BIR EIYUB)

The second ancient natural water source in the Jerusalem area is that known today as Bir Eiyub, or in English, Job's Well. It lies just below the junction of the Hinnom and the Kidron valleys, a little way off from the city, and has never been enclosed by a city wall. It is thus not as accessible a water source as the Virgin's Fountain but is more regular and has often been used as a last resort in times of drought.

There has been some controversy over the origin and nature of Job's Well, particularly as to whether or not it is a true well or an underground spring.[2] It is 125 feet deep and taps the lower Turonian rocks at its base. As its sources of water are from a wider area than those of the Virgin's Fountain, because of the depth of the strata tapped, it gives a more reliable flow of water, even in summer. It seems unlikely that it taps just a gathering of surface waters, although if streams ever flow down the Kidron and Hinnom, this is the place where they tend to disappear beneath the surface as the limestone absorbs them. The well seems, however, to draw water from the lower Turonian layers, resting on top of Cenomanian rocks which, restricting downward percolation of water, cause it to "flow" along the more pervious strata. Sir Charles Wilson noticed the water "weeping" into the well when it was fairly empty. The existence of a spring here originally, is unlikely in view of the dip of the strata. Lack of knowledge of this stratification may have deceived many early scholars. It is most likely that here in old times, pools of water were formed after torrents had flowed down the valleys and a well was dug to tap this water. As the well got deeper, it struck a more constant flow at the base of the meleke layers. Thus Job's Well is a deep well tapping underground water and not a deepened spring, and around it has developed a small hamlet and gardens. Edward Robinson described this place as "the prettiest and most fertile around Jerusalem" and it repre-sents the last spot of green in the valley on its journey down to the Dead Sea.

There are some problems in the identification of Job's Well with Biblical names. It is undoubtedly ancient, and a number of old aqueducts and tunnels lead off from the well or around it.

---

2 G. A. Smith, *Jerusalem*, Vol. II, pp. 98-100.

It is generally identified with En Rogel, although as has been seen, many older scholars attached this name to the Virgin's Fountain. We know however, from II Samuel 17:17 that En Rogel was out of sight of the city and if Zion be on Ophel, then the location of Job's Well is preferable to that of the Virgin's Fountain. En Rogel is also mentioned as a point on the border of Judah, in Joshua 15:7-8, which seems to rule out the Virgin's Fountain and support an identification with Job's Well. This well has also been identified with the Dragon Well of Nehemiah 2:13, although with the modern legend of a dragon attached to the Virgin's Fountain it is tempting to regard this as an alternative name for the latter. The main objection to an identification of Job's Well as En Rogel is in the name which implies that it is a spring. There is no definite or decisive evidence on the problem, but most scholars now consider Job's Well to be identical with En Rogel and the Virgin's Fountain to be Gihon.

POOL OF SILOAM AND HEZEKIAH'S TUNNEL

The hydrological system of the Pool of Siloam and Hezekiah's Tunnel is the first of the artificial water sources to be dealt with, in view of its close connection with the Virgin's Fountain. At the mouth of the Tyropoeon valley are two ancient pools, one above the other and surrounded by a number of trees. The lower and larger of these pools, which is now filled in, is known as Birket el Hamra or the Old Pool. Above this is a now smaller tank known as Birket Silwan or the Pool of Siloam. The source of water for this pool is the Virgin's Fountain, the water passing through a circuitous tunnel. The need for a source of water near the mouth of the Tyropoeon valley was probably a result of the insecurity attached to the Virgin's Fountain, which lay outside the walls and even through Warren's Shaft access was very difficult. In addition, the city seems to have spread out from its original site on the summit of Ophel, into the Tyropoeon and onto the western hill, thus rendering the spring a long way from the newer residential quarters and a source in the Tyropoeon would be much more central. Birket el Hamra, probably represents an early attempt to provide a more accessible water supply by catching surface run-off in the valley, as it is dammed by a wall which is undoubtedly old. It is quite likely, as some scholars have maintained, that it received water from the old aqueduct which led from the Virgin's Fountain around the spur of Ophel on the surface. This system may well have been the "waters of Shiloah that go softly" (Isa. 8:6). We also get mention of a Pool of Shelah here in Nehemiah (3:7). Whatever the date of the original water works here, we know that Hezekiah constructed a system to divert the water from outside the walls into the city in order to deprive the Assyrians of water and to safeguard his own supplies. The present tunnel which carries water from the Virgin's Fountain to the Pool of Siloam is undoubtedly the tunnel built by Hezekiah to divert the water. An inscription found in it in 1880 dates the tunnel to pre-Exilic times and Hezekiah's works are the only ones we know of on this scale. It was in fact a magnificent piece of engineering, as few mistakes were made in direction, and the large curves which the tunnel takes are almost certainly deliberate, although controversy still rages as to their purpose.

The location of the pools at the southern end of the Tyropoeon valley would make this area an important focal point in the old city and it is quite possible that an early market or public open space was located here. The Pool of Siloam has remained in use since its original construction and is also a minor center of pilgrimages. An old church was excavated over the pool and it is mentioned by the Bordeaux Pilgrim and St. Jerome. It is interesting that the latter mentions that it is the only fountain in Jerusalem, and Josephus refers to it as a spring. This rather suggests that in folk memory, the connection between the pool and the Virgin's Fountain became lost and the pool was regarded as a spring in its own right. The pool has shared the same irregularity of supply as its source, the Virgin's Fountain, and the level of water can vary greatly. Although Josephus refers to its waters as sweet, organic matter of sewage derivation has been found in it, but the pool continues in use by the local population.

The Pool of Siloam is now 50 x 15 feet in dimension, but Bliss, who excavated the area, considered it to have diminished in size since its first construction, through the amount of building on and around it. The tunnel is 533 meters long from spring to the entrance to the pool with a gradient of 1:250 on the average. The slope is not constant, however, and there are parts of the tunnel where the water can be very deep.

POOL OF BETHESDA (ST. ANNE'S)

The modern pool to which the name "Bethesda" is generally given is a pool, with another parallel to it, which lies behind the Church of St. Anne, just inside St. Stephen's Gate. In site it is very interesting because it lies in the hidden valley tributary to the Kidron which was only discovered when Warren plumbed the rock contours under the city's debris. This area just north of the Haram enclosure is one which contains a number of tanks and pools of all ages. The Pool of Bethesda is 55 x 12½ feet in dimension, with a small amount of water near the bottom. As it lies in the St. Anne's valley, it may originally have been intended as a tank to catch surface run-off, but the main source of water now appears to be rainfall. There is no trace of a spring, nor is one likely as the surface rock is entirely Turonian meleke. It is possible that in periods of high rainfall there may be some seepage into the pool from the rock beds into which it is built, but the source today seems to be entirely rain.

As a pool, it is certainly ancient and was built over in Crusader times with churches. It is quite likely to be the twin pools mentioned by Jerome and the Burgundian Pilgrim as the ones then pointed out to be the Pool of Bethesda, but it was buried under debris for many centuries and only saw the light of day again in 1871. Since then excavations have revealed extensive Byzantine and Crusader remains. It is not used as a water source today, but is quite a tourist attraction.

Whether this is the Pool of Bethesda mentioned in John 5:2 is difficult to say with certainty. The apostle does give us some information with regard to the pool which helps, but it does not completely fit the pool behind St. Anne's. We read that the Pool of Bethesda had five porches and that it had connections with sheep (a gate or market) and was "troubled" periodically. Now the pool at St. Anne's has the porches and is near the Gate of St. Stephen (Bab Siiti Mariam) which is considered by many to be the old Sheep Gate. Another clue as to location is in the name "Bethesda." This name is not found elsewhere than in John 5:2, but in some versions of Eusebius, it is corrupted to Bezatha, which is very like "Bezetha," which was the name given to the new quarter in the northern part of Jerusalem, mentioned by Josephus. Whether the original was *Beth-esda* or *Beth-zeit* is a matter for conjecture, but it could be that the pool and the district had the same name. A matter of great uncertainty is the "troubling" of the waters. This would suggest a spring or other intrusion which does not exist at the St. Anne's Pool, which is as placid as the proverbial 'mill pool.' The pool of Birket Israel, which was for many centuries pointed out as the Pool of Bethesda, has no such feature either and neither have the pools under the Sisters of Zion convent. The Virgin's Fountain

REMAINS OF AN OLD CHURCH which was built over the supposed site of the Pool of Bethesda.

comes to mind, of course, with its famous turbulence, and there
has been some discussion as to the possibilities of there being a
pool in the Kidron in front of this spring. It has been suggested
that Bethesda might be here, especially as the spring is not
mentioned as such in the New Testament, and it is the only
place in Jerusalem where this disturbance of the water occurs.
However, in all other respects the St. Anne's pool seems to have
the better claim.

BIRKET ISRAEL AND THE TWIN POOLS

South of the pool in the St. Anne enclosure and lower down
the hidden valley lies a large pool, now covered over, known
as Birket Israel. Its origin is unknown, for although it has ancient characteristics, it is not mentioned by Josephus, despite its
size of 360 x 126 feet. It appears to fill naturally by run-off
and some pipes and drains lead from it. The pool rests on the
northern wall of the Haram enclosure with a masonry dam having Roman characteristics and is lined with cement. It was probably the pool identified by mediaeval pilgrims as the Pool of
Bethesda but there is no evidence of porticos and it was probably so identified because it was the largest pool then visible in
the area of the old Sheep Gate.

West of this pool, under the present Sisters of Zion convent,
are two pools often called the Twin Pools. They adjoin what
was the northwest corner of the Antonia fortress and have interesting connections, for an aqueduct leads into them from the
north, passing east of the Damascus Gate and another flows
eastward to a small tank under the barracks west of the Birket
Israel. Although these Twin Pools were identified with Josephus'
Pool Strouthion by Clermont Ganneau and Vincent, some scholars have considered them to be the Bethesda of the mediaeval
pilgrims.

BIRKET ES-SULTAN

This large reservoir, now dry, is probably not as old as the
ones previously mentioned. It stands in the Wadi er-Rababi or
Hinnom, just west of the southwest corner of the Old City wall
and was probably originally built to catch the water from the
periodic streams which run down this valley after heavy rain.
Charles Wilson considered that it was also an overflow tank for
the Low Level Aqueduct. It is 55 x 220 feet in size and was
repaired in the sixteenth century and so must have been in use
in the early part of the Ottoman period, but by the nineteenth

century it had declined to the status of a cattle market and today lies waste. Its significance as a feature of the urban geography of Jerusalem is thus confined to the Arab and Ottoman periods.

BIRKET HAMMAM AL-BATRAK (PATRIARCH'S BATH)

This pool is known in English as the Pool of the Patriarch's Bath (or Hezekiah's Pool from the older views on the location of Gihon, Zion and the Kidron) and is located inside the Old City within the Christian Quarter. It may be quite ancient and has been identified with the pool Amygdalon of Josephus, but is not used much today. It was explored by Conrad Schick in the last century and measures 240 x 144 feet in area and is about 20 feet deep. It appears that originally it may have extended further to the north as the cement floor of the pool extends in that direction. The source of water seems to be entirely rainfall, but in ancient times it received water from the High Level aqueduct.

Several other pools exist in the city including a large number of cisterns. Indeed, to judge by the number of these cisterns, it appears that every building in the Old City has at some time had a private source of water, usually from rainwater collected from the roof. This source is not very hygienic but was the main supply for the inhabitants until the Royal Engineers built an aqueduct into the city in 1918. A large cistern of this type is the Hammam esh-Shafa, just south of the Suk al Kattanin and west of the Haram enclosure, which is now buried under buildings. The Haram area contains a number of tanks and cisterns, many linked in a complicated system. The source of most of the water in the Haram enclosure, apart from rainfall, was the aqueduct from Solomon's Pools. Outside the Old City, higher up the Wadi er Rababi, is the Birket Mamilla, a large pool (292 x 193 feet) of uncertain age which now forms part of a park in the Israeli part of the city.

EXTERNAL SUPPLIES

Jerusalem's water supply has been generally adequate in years of ample rainfall and as long as the population was kept fairly low. However, during times of prosperity when the population increased or after prolonged drought, other sources have been sought, for it is obvious that a city the size of that of Herod the Great or the present Old City, could not rely on Job's Well as a last resort. Consequently, from quite early times efforts have been made to bring in water from outside in order to ensure a regular supply. This, of course, is not easy and neither is it cheap. An aqueduct has to be carefully planned, kept in repair and cleaned, and it presents an easy target for an enemy. Consequently, the periods of aqueduct building in Jerusalem have been those of maximum security and strong government.

The first two long range aqueducts were constructed in the first century A.D. or just before. These are known as the High Level and the Low Level aqueducts. The High Level aqueduct began in the Wadi el Biar from an ancient reservoir and disgorged within the Old City in the Birket Hammam al Batrak. Although using mainly gravity for its flow, this aqueduct did employ an inverted syphon to cross a valley near Bethlehem, which, together with the fact that it appears to have emptied near Herod's palace gardens, has tended to date the aqueduct to the time of that king's reign. Its purpose is more likely to have been the securing of the king's supplies of water rather than those of the populace.

Similarly, the Low Level aqueduct was not primarily for public consumption except in times of dire need, for it ended up within the Temple area to feed the tanks there. This aqueduct ran from Solomon's Pools, which were fed by channels bringing water from neighboring springs, under gravity, a distance of twenty-five miles. Major F. W. Stephen estimated that at the end of the First World War, this aqueduct carried 80,000 gallons of water each day, half of which arrived at Jerusalem and the rest went to Bethlehem.[3] Of that which arrived at Jerusalem, some disgorged into the Birket es-Sultan (foul water) and the rest found its way to the Haram area. This aqueduct ensured an external supply to the city, but its usefulness was limited by its exit points, i.e. at the Birket es-Sultan, which was not a hygienic source, and the Haram. There was no water within easy access of the inhabitants and the aqueduct could not discharge at a higher level than 2430 feet. One can only assume that in most years the inhabitants found sufficient supplies from their cisterns and tanks.

Modern water came to Jerusalem in 1918. Although many schemes had been suggested to improve the supply of water before (Charles Wilson's famous plan of the city had been surveyed for such a scheme), and the Ottoman government had repaired the aqueduct from Solomon's Pools in the sixteenth

3 F. W. Stephen, *P.E.Q.* (1919).

century, nothing radical had been done since the time of Pilate when the Low Level aqueduct was built. After the British had taken the city, however, a new source was opened up from the hills to the west of Jerusalem. It yielded 14,000 gallons an hour and the old cisterns and tanks were cleaned out and filled with fresh water. Now practically the whole supply of water is piped from outside, although there are still a number of tanks and cisterns in use and the Virgin's Fountain and the Pool of Siloam are still used by local inhabitants.

The water supply of Jerusalem can be seen to be very varied. With the tanks and cisterns full and the aqueducts flowing, the city must have felt well supplied, and Mukaddasi, one of Jerusalem's most famous sons, wrote "There is water in Jerusalem in plenty. Thus it is a common saying that there is no place in Jerusalem but where you may get water and hear the call to prayer; and few are the houses that have not cisterns — one or more." It is these cisterns, whose total capacity was once estimated at 360 million gallons, which have provided the main source of supply down the centuries until the present time, but now with an increasing population and better hygienic standards the time will no doubt come when they will be entirely replaced by the piped supplies.

IV

THE CITY ECONOMY

One of the distinctive features of an urban community is the multiplicity of economic activities which are found there for even in a holy city a large proportion of the population earn their living by manufacturing or selling the necessities and luxuries of life or give some service which is paid for in cash. This confusion of activity often makes it difficult to determine what are the "functions" of a city and on what economic base it originated and developed. In this chapter the economy of Jerusalem will be surveyed generally and in the following chapter the pilgrim/tourist industry will be looked at in more detail as this is certainly the most important and distinctive feature of the city's commercial life.

The origins of Jerusalem are lost in the distant past so it is difficult to say whether the city first arose as a defensive point commanding routes through the Hill Country or as a market town, or was perhaps even in pre-Jewish days, a religious sanctuary. Frequent mention of commercial activities in the Bible suggest that this element was present very early, but sooner or later the religious activity influenced all other sectors of the economy. The economic flow diagram opposite illustrates the interaction of the various parts of the economic life of Jerusalem. It shows the flow of money from the main spending sources, i.e. tourism, government, and the surrounding populace, into the commercial life of the city and through to the sectors involved in primary production. Thus, to take just one of the spending chains, tourists spend a major proportion of their money on hotel accommodation. This money in turn is spent on food, staff wages, maintenance, etc. Thus the hotel industry keeps much of the food retailing sector in business. In turn this provides a livelihood to the food wholesalers and processing industries (bakers, food packers, etc.) and this in turn provides a market for the farmers of the neighborhood. This sort of chain can be repeated throughout the model. Of course it should be emphasized that it is very much oversimplified and in actual fact is much more complicated than might appear from the model. For example, many of the food retailers are also processors and some hotels buy direct from the wholesaler or producer. In addition, the model is based upon present conditions, but in previous ages, the picture might have been different. It does however, illustrate how the separate parts of the economy of Jerusalem are linked together and in particular the extent to which the tourist sector influences the rest. The various sectors will now be examined in turn and their relative importance assessed.

PRIMARY PRODUCTION

Agriculture

Writers have expressed conflicting opinions on the fertility of the Jerusalem district, depending on the origin and experiences

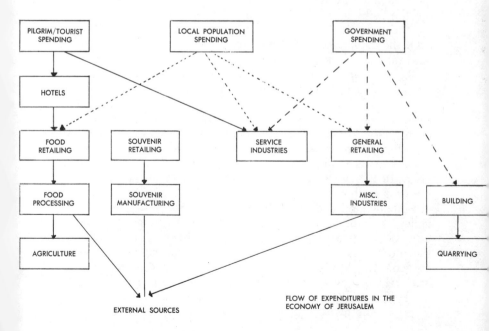

FLOW OF EXPENDITURES IN THE
ECONOMY OF JERUSALEM

of the writer. Many have been very complimentary. Palestine as a whole was described by the Jews in the Exodus wanderings as "a good land, a land of brooks of water, of fountains and depths, springing forth in valleys and hills; a land of wheat and barley and vines and fig trees and pomegranates; a land of oil olives and honey . . ." (Deut. 8:7-8). Felix Fabri considered that in the Jerusalem area "all the necessities of life grow there in abundance," while Mukaddasi considered the city very productive and mentions oranges, bananas, and almonds among the produce grown. Yet others have been less pleased and Warburton commented that "not a tree or green spot is visible." Nevertheless there are very fertile and prosperous valleys in the vicinity, even if at times the hills have a very barren appearance. Niccolo of Poggibonsi perhaps sums it up best: "Its surroundings have neither forests nor wood; fruit trees and vineyards there are in plenty and its soil is very precious; and all is hills, mounts and valleys." Generally the hills have remained barren, but the large demand for food from the city has helped to maintain an intense agriculture in some of the surrounding valleys and even within the city walls there is some cultivation in gardens. Thus it is not inappropriate to include a section on agriculture in a book on a city, for no one can visit Jerusalem without being aware of the cultivated patches within and without the Old City or of the flocks of sheep and goats which nibble the grass on the banks which flank the city walls.

Of the main agricultural products of the area, *the olive* is perhaps the best known. It has many uses, varying from fuel (Matt. 25:3), medicine (Luke 10:34) and hairdressing to a raw material in soap manufacture and even as timber (I Kings 6:23). There was a considerable demand for olive oil in the city because it was a major source of power, and at times there has been a large export. The Jerusalem area has in fact a considerable reputation in olive production and there are many testimonies to its richness in this crop even when other crops are poor. In Byzantine times there was a widespread production of the crop in this area. Arculfus noticed a "great wood of olives" at Bethany, and Bede records the existence of olive groves in the valleys west of Jerusalem. In the Middle Ages under the stimulus of a great demand for oil for heating and lighting, the production of olives flourished and large harvests were recorded. The Mount of Olives was once covered with the trees after which it was named, although now larger trees dominate the landscape. Olive trees also flourished in the Bethlehem area. There seems to have been a decline in production during the

Ottoman period, for Niebuhr noticed few trees, but there was still a considerable number in the nineteenth century.

The vine is another old crop in this area, receiving frequent mention in the ancient literature. It has, however, had a checkered career; for although it was valued by Jews and Christians, Moslem tradition forbade its use and it suffered under Moslem rule, especially when Hakem had a large number of the trees destroyed. It is well suited to the hills and foothills and the deep roots enable it to survive in areas of low rainfall. To judge by Isaiah's prophecies, the Jerusalem area must have been productive in vines in early times (Isa. 7:23), and there are many place-names indicating its cultivation. Today it can be seen in many places around, and especially along the road to Hebron. In Byzantine times and even early Arab times the vine seems to have flourished in the district, for both Bede and Mukaddasi comment on their production, and Joannes Phocas found the hill opposite the Tower of David full of vines. It seems to have generally declined since Hakem's onslaught, however, and is not as widespread as formerly.

Figs were ubiquitous in ancient times but do not appear to have been particularly important in the Jerusalem area. They were grown near Bethany at one time, and Robinson mentions seeing them in the Siloam gardens. Suriano also mentions figs in the vicinity of the city, but otherwise there are comparatively few references to them. They are not common today.

Cereals are rarely mentioned in connection with Jerusalem, as the Hill Country is not ideal for their cultivation. Only small patches in the valleys were sown with wheat or barley, which were apparently grown in the Bethlehem area in ancient times, for they are mentioned in the Book of Ruth (2:23). Wheat seems to have been Boaz's main crop (Ruth 2:3). Theodorich noticed corn growing in the Jerusalem area, but references are not common and little can be seen in the district at the present time.

A variety of fruit and vegetables were cultivated in the Jerusalem area, including nuts (especially almonds), pomegranates, and apples. The Mishnah even mentions roses. Josephus mentions chick-peas as a crop. Mushrooms have also been grown. This intensive cultivation in close proximity to the city in Jewish times, enabled farmers to use blood from the Temple sacrifices as fertilizer. There have always been many gardens in and around the city and also attempts at fish culture in the Pool of Siloam.

The rearing of livestock is not common in the immediate

proximity to cities, but nevertheless Jerusalem even today seems to attract goats and sheep which graze on its wastes. At one time flocks grazed in the Garden of Gethsemane according to Ludolph of Suchem, and there are a number of flocks using the Mount of Olives and the area to the south of the Old City. Most of these animals are probably destined for the city butchers, although there is a small market for dairy produce today and some small dairy herds are kept in the district.

Quarrying and Lumbering

The Jerusalem area was once rich in wood but with the considerable usage of this valuable material in building and sieges (especially that of Titus), the timber resources of Jerusalem have been depleted. Shortage of timber considerably hindered the Crusaders in their attempts to take the city, and it will be recalled that Solomon, although he used local olive wood, also had to send to Lebanon for the better quality timber. Quarrying has been a prosperous extractive industry in the area in view of the demand for building stone. Public buildings from Solomon's Temple to the present day constructions west of the city,

BETHLEHEM. Sheep following their shepherd. Courtesy, Levant Photo Service

have demanded large quantities of stone and the numerous quarries in the district, notably those known as Solomon's Quarries, bear witness to this activity. The decision of the Mandate authorities, upheld by the Israel and Jordanian governments to use only local stone (not concrete or brick) on buildings within Jerusalem, has meant a continued prosperity for this industry.

SECONDARY PRODUCTION

Unlike many of the manufacturing cities of Europe and North America, Jerusalem has no major manufacturing industry which dwarfs all others. There are instead many small industries using local or imported raw materials and producing, usually in family units, commodities for local consumption or for the tourist industry. It should be noted that often retail and productive aspects of an industry are combined in one concern, but at the same time there has been little development of large firms controlling a sizable part of the market, but rather the commercial life of the city is still as it has always been in the hands of small family firms.

Food processing is not very important, but certain industries are quite strong and serve generally a local market. Bakers have been in Jerusalem for many centuries, for Josephus records that there were some attached to the Temple and there were special bakers to produce the shew bread. Confectionery is a strong trade at the present time, and is especially found in small shops in the Suq Khan es-Zeit in producer-retailer establishments. Bread and confectionary items have been vital commodities to the population in the past, and in Mamluk times regulations were in force to ensure a supply of flour and bread to the city. *Oil milling* was common, as might be expected from what has been said of the cultivation of the olive. The strength of the industry can be judged by the requirement of the Haram area for one hundred kists of oil a month and with the good local sources of supply the industry flourished. Naturally, with the advent of electricity as a source of power and fuel, the production of olive oil has declined although to some extent its place has been taken over by soap manufacture. Another processing industry has been wine making although this is not carried on in the city at the present time.

One of the major secondary industries is that of souvenir manufacture. We read early in the Old Testament of precious metals and gems being required for the worship of Jehovah (Ex. 35:27). Gold was used extensively in Solomon's Temple (I Kings 6:21-22) so that the metals industry had an early start, and it is fairly certain that much of its production would have been in the form of souvenirs or religious objects for personal use. In Roman times the smiths had a special market in the city, and religious accessories such as perfumes, ointments, incense, etc., were produced in the city as well as imported. Thus we get an early development of "luxury" industries, dependent on the Temple and the religious activities of Jerusalem. Later in Christian times, the development of a souvenir industry proper can be seen. In the Byzantine era, there were large profits in relic manufacture and Jerusalem became famous for its rosaries. According to the author of *Citez de Jherusalem* (13th century), goldsmiths worked a lively trade.

However, the real developments on the manufacturing side of the souvenir industry came in the sixteenth century, when the Franciscans began in earnest to foster the pilgrim trade. Bernardino Amico, who did much to help develop this industry, has left a considerable amount of information about it. Bethlehem was at first a larger center for manufacturing than was Jerusalem, and it still produces a large number of objects from mother-of-pearl and olive wood. In 1586, its population was engaged in making rosaries and crosses of wood, but because this did not flourish as was hoped (there were criticisms of rough work), the mother-of-pearl industry was begun and has never looked back. With the help of the plans of churches which Amico had made, reproductions were made in stone and sold to visitors and apparently the industry prospered, for Amico reports that "so they buy their food, dividing among them the profits." Some of this work was exported to Europe by the Franciscans. Today, a bewildering selection of souvenirs greets the pilgrim, many made by small family firms. Large numbers are employed in this way.[1]

Another old industry is the *building industry*, which has prospered particularly in Jerusalem because of the large number of churches and public buildings which have been erected from time to time. The first great impetus to the industry undoubtedly came in Solomon's reign with the building of the Temple, although earlier carpenters and masons had been employed on the building of David's house (II Sam. 5:11). The

---

1 See *Hashemite Kingdom of Jordon, Statistical Handbook* (1964), p. 57.

Bible records that 30,000 men were employed in building the Temple, with 3,300 officers over the work (I Kings 5:13, 16). This must have been an enormous injection into the economy, although one can imagine the unemployment which probably resulted when the work was completed. However, some skilled men were probably kept on as a permanent repair team, for we read of repairs under Joash (II Kings 12:11). The second period of great building activity occurred during the restoration under Nehemiah when masons and carpenters as well as more casual labor were employed in the Temple work (Ezra 3:7). The building projects of Herod the Great must have kept the industry occupied for many years, and in Byzantine times the large numbers of churches constructed probably gave another impetus to the building industry. Again, we have records that in normal times a certain labor force was kept on repair work. Extensive repairs were undertaken to the Dome of the Rock in the sixteenth century and also in the 1960's. Recently extensive work has been undertaken on the Holy Sepulcher Church. In

CALVARY. The entrance to the Holy Sepulcher. The Chapel of Calvary is inside to the right.

the last hundred years the excavations of various archaeologists required large amounts of labor.[2]

Another strong industry in Jerusalem has been that concerned with textiles and leather. The leather industry is common in most cities in the Middle East, Jerusalem having no particular locational advantages. The industry is mentioned by some mediaeval pilgrims because of the Moslem habit of placing tanning plants, which give off a very obnoxious smell, in close proximity to Christian holy sites. Weavers were attached to the Temple in classical times and Maundrell many centuries later noticed a weaver's workshop in the Place of Scourging. Weaving was one of the industries encouraged by the Pro-Jerusalem Society and soon after the Second World War, the "Jerusalem Looms" employed seventy people. Fulling seems to have been an ancient craft in Jerusalem, as a fullers' field is mentioned in the Old Testament (II Kings 18:17), and ancient fullers' vats were found near Job's Well. Dyeing was widespread in ancient times and in the Middle Ages. Benjamin of Tudela mentions the industry at Bethlehem. There was also a cotton printing industry in Jerusalem in the early nineteenth century.

The soap industry has received a brief mention, and need not be dwelt on in detail for the main center of the industry now is Nablus. However, Robinson noted that in his time, with nine establishments operating, soap manufacture was the chief industry of the city. Today a large amount of oil is produced in the Jerusalem district. Other industries in the city include that of candle making, pottery production, and the tile industry, the latter being another line encouraged by the Pro-Jerusalem Council.

Retailing and Service Industries

While the general impression gained of Jerusalem by the visitor is not that of an industrial city, there is no doubt that commerce abounds. Shops and hawkers, taxi drivers and guides, greet one every step of the way from hotel to the Holy Sepulcher. The retailing and service industries are now recognized as important elements in the study of urban geography because of their large contributions to the economic and social life of any town. Because of their need for an ideal location and the relatively high profits which can be obtained, retailing tends to be

2 See for example, F. J. Bliss and A. C. Dickie, *Excavations at Jerusalem, 1894-1897*, p. 339.

one of the main elements in determining land prices and can
have a great influence on any community. In Oriental cities,
especially those which have remained little touched by modern
influences, retailing tends to be fragmented, with nothing re-
sembling the modern chain store but rather a mosaic of small
family concerns all in hot competition. Frequent mention is
made of the markets and fairs in the pilgrim accounts of the
city in the Middle Ages and it seems that merchants from all
over the Mediterranean world converged on Jerusalem to profit
from these occasions. At one time it became close to being
an international trading center, and there was much export of
cheese, cotton, raisins, apples, bananas, etc. Even the Pope's
ban on pilgrimages to the Holy Land did not stop the Venetian
traders. It is probably the merchant pilgrims who began this
process, unable to resist doing a bit of trade while saving their
souls and, in any case, the gatherings at Easter and Christmas
were convenient meetings between East and West.

Souvenir selling was of course a prosperous form of retailing
with the inhabitants, although some religious bodies have done
and do engage in it also. Relics were popular at one time and
large amounts of local earth were taken back to Europe by zeal-
ous pilgrims. Fragments of the Golden Gate were sold for two
ducats each![3] The modern pilgrim makes do with slides and
postcards instead. Religious ornaments were sold, and towards
the end of the Middle Ages there was a wide trade in mother-
of-pearl and olive wood objects. The convents joined in this
trade with force and Lamartine noted that the Latin convent
sold crosses, chaplets, etc. Today, the trade is widespread
and much the same type of object is sold, i.e. crucifixes, rosaries,
with the addition of wooden camels and a considerable amount
of embroidery work.

Mention has already been made of textile production, so it
is not surprising to discover that there was and is a large retail
business in this line. Mediaeval accounts inform us that "stuffs,"
safron, mastic and drapery were sold in the city and at one time
there was a cotton bazaar. Most of the shops are small ones in the
covered suq although there are now a number of modern
tailors and fashion shops to the north and west of the Old City.
Most of the customers are local inhabitants, but there is some
trade with tourists, especially with the fancier silk and decora-
tive items.

A large part of the retailing activity is concerned with the

---

3 Frescobaldi, *Visit in the Holy Places* (1384), p. 71.

selling of food and this is the dominant line in the Suq Khan es-Zeit. There is some evidence of a lively trade in wheat in early times (I Kings 5:11; Prov. 11:26), and in the Middle Ages corn was sold near the Tower of David. Fish was sold in the city by Tyrians at the time of the return from exile (Neh. 13:16), and there was a Fish Gate in the northern wall. In the Middle Ages there was a large supply of fish from the Sea of Galilee on which the canons of the Holy Sepulcher had rights during the time of the Latin Kingdom. The Roman Catholic consumption of fish instead of meat on Fridays has helped in keeping this trade alive, although obtaining fresh fish was not easy in the Arab sector of the city from 1948 to 1967. The meat trade is also active and there are many butchers in the Old City suqs. Frequent mention of meat retailing is made in the pilgrim accounts of the Middle Ages and there must have been a considerable consumption during the times of the great Christian feasts. Herbs and spices have been sold in the city for a long time, and there was a special street devoted to this trade at one time. Cheese selling is mentioned in *Citez de Jherusalem* and if the name Tyropoeon or Valley of Cheesemakers is taken at its face value, then there must have been some trade in this item in Biblical times, but in general the Middle East has never seen the development of a large dairy retailing trade as is the case in Europe or North America. There has been a larger trade in vegetables and fruit, which have been the staple items in the diet of local inhabitants. At the present time there are a large number of vegetable stalls in a special market off David Street which provides the greater part of the needs of the hotels in East Jerusalem.

Mention should be made of the service industries which have often been very important in Jerusalem. At the present time the chief service activities are those of the guides (official and unofficial!) and the taxis. The former trade is quite old and was noted by Felix Fabri and has tended to descend in families, the art being passed on from father to son. To many of the young boys of Jerusalem, their main ambition is to become a guide. Tattooing has been practiced in the city up to the present time and Maundrell observed the art being executed in the Holy Sepulcher on Easter Saturday.

HOTELS AND CATERING

One of the most important industries in Jerusalem is the hotel business. It is very old, for the Jewish pilgrims in Biblical times must have needed somewhere to stay. If there was an inn at Bethlehem, then there must have been several at Jerusalem. The "upper room" of the Last Supper may in fact have been a lodging house. In the Byzantine era there were a number of hospices. Justinian built one, and Fetellus mentions a Xenodochium or hospice for the sick and travelers. A large number of hospices flourished in Mediaeval times and a large number of khans, for use by native visitors, were in existence, including one large one called Al-Wakala in Mamluk times. At one time there was a large hospice on the site of the Order of St. John of Jerusalem which held one thousand pilgrims and charged a flat rate of two Venetian pennies per person irrespective of length of stay. The Franciscan convent, originally on Mt. Zion, was mentioned by many western pilgrims, and there was also a large one for Armenians, taking three to four thousand pilgrims. A Coptic khan was built in 1838, but the great hotel building period did not begin until the end of the nineteenth century when the numbers of visitors from Europe began to increase to large proportions. Since the last war, there has been an unprecedented development to meet the ever increasing numbers of tourists, and in the Jordanian part of the city particularly a large number of high class hotels have appeared to the north of the city and on the Mount of Olives. The hospices and hostels are, however, still doing a good trade, often catering to particular nationalities or religious beliefs. Thus Roman Catholic pilgrims tend to go to the Casa Nova hospice, British and American Protestants to St. George's or Christ Church, Greeks to their convent near the Holy Sepulcher, etc.

In addition to overnight accommodations, there has been a large street catering sector. In the Middle Ages there was a special street where food was cooked for pilgrims, and in the 16th century we read of attempts to establish coffee houses, despite government disapproval. Today, a large number of cafés and soft drink stalls do a roaring trade.

FINANCIAL ACTIVITY

With all the other commercial and industrial activity already mentioned, as well as the large numbers of foreign and native pilgrims, it is not surprising to see rather extensive financial activity in the city. As far back as pre-Exilic times, the Temple was being used as a bank. When Ahaz "took the silver and gold that was found in the house of the Lord, and in the treasures of the king's house, and sent it for a present to the king of Assyria," it need not be assumed that this was a case of robbing the Temple, for that building quite likely served as a state reserve bank as well as keeping the valuables of individuals. This was quite a normal function for temples in this part of the world, where often only the priests were literate and could keep accounts. Money changers also appear at an early date, using the Temple precincts to change the money of the pilgrims from the Diaspora (Matt. 21:12). In the Middle Ages there was an exchange at the southeast corner of the Muristan, and today there is also a large number scattered throughout the city who change the travelers checks of a multitude of nations into cash.

GOVERNMENT ACTIVITY

In addition to its function as a trading center and marketplace for the surrounding villages, and in connection with the pilgrim/tourist trade, Jerusalem has also had the important function as a seat of government. With the vast expenditures which governments can make, this factor has further injected a considerable amount of money into the city's economy. The importance of Jerusalem as a center of government has, of course, varied with its status. It has at times been the capital of a vast area, but at other periods it has been just a small regional center, a cog in a larger machine. The city has certain advantages for administration. In the first place, the original site on Ophel was an extremely good defensive point and made it an attractive site in ancient times when it was often necessary to stop work in order to repel invaders. Any capital in times of uncertainty had to be easily defended. In addition, Jerusalem has advantages of centrality. Although, as has been pointed out, the city is not on any major routes and has no easy access, it is central to Western Palestine and in particular to the Hill Country. The functions which a capital city engages in are largely military and administrative. As a military base, Jerusalem has often been used to subdue the Hill Country and has seen armies quartered in it. In Crusader times the Knights Templar and other orders lived in the city, which at times resembled a military camp. Similarly at the present time it is alive with Israeli soldiers using it as a base for the subjection of the West Bank of Jordan. Administrative functions have included the collection of taxes and the administration of justice, and there has always been a certain amount of ecclesiastical administration emanating from the city. In Jewish times, the Sanhedrin was strong and the High Priest held quasi-governmental powers, while in Mediaeval and

Ottoman times the city was used by a number of religious orders and bishops as a headquarters.

The strength of the administrative element in the life of Jerusalem has varied in time, and hence the amount of money spent in the city by government agencies has also varied. During the empire of David and Solomon the city was a royal stronghold and must have received visitors from all over the Empire coming to see the king on business or to seek justice or pay taxes. A large garrison was kept by David and this no doubt created a considerable demand for food. An early civil service was set up, headed it seems by Zadok the priest, Nathan the prophet, and Benaiah the son of Jehoiada (I Kings 1:32). All this affected the economy by increasing the food market and probably fostering a rudimentary hotel industry. The building programs of the government were also large, for apart from the Temple there was the building of the king's house (II Sam. 5: 11) and the Millo (II Sam. 5:9), as well as repairs to the defenses. All these expenditures, paid for ultimately by the taxpayer, fostered economic development. Considerable growth in the city's wealth and population were witnessed with a considerable rise in the cost of living. This whole period seems to have been a happy one, for "Judah and Israel were many, as the sand which is by the sea in multitude, eating and drinking and making merry" (I Kings 4:20). Some idea of the importance of governmental demands in the economy can be obtained by reading of the daily provisions of Solomon's court in I Kings 4:21-28. The provision was thirty measures of fine flour, sixty measures of meal, ten fat oxen, twenty oxen "out of the pastures," one hundred sheep, plus harts, gazelles, roebucks and fatted fowl. This amount of consumption by the government must have brought about a very healthy trading sector and the chronicler, after discussing the amount of tribute which came in to Solomon (666 talents of gold) each year, says that "the king made silver to be in Jerusalem as stones" (II Chron. 9:27). The complaints, made after Solomon's death, that he overtaxed the nation and overspent are likely to be the grumblings of the middle classes who always feel taxation more than others, for it is doubtful if Solomon really did overspend. His actions certainly injected a considerable amount of money into the economy and raised Jerusalem from a small Hill Country market town to a rich capital, and his public works must have created considerable employment and private wealth. Such government expenditure is regarded as quite normal in underdeveloped countries today and was wiser than spending large amounts of taxation on the maintenance of a large army to keep the empire intact. Solomon's wisdom may have stretched to some rudimentary economics!

After the collapse of the first Jewish empire, Jerusalem's status declined and successive governments had not the wealth to continue the support of the economy which Solomon had done. It is to be assumed therefore that the city returned to a normal growth level and that government expenditures gave way more and more to private expenditures. Under Nehemiah, the city governed only a very small area, although with the vast rebuilding programs of the new provincial government, there must have been little unemployment. As the city became the capital of a larger area under the Hasmonaeans and eventually under Herod the Great, more government activity was seen. The building program of Herod undoubtedly brought much wealth to Jerusalem. Although Caesarea was the official Roman capital and Herod tried to avoid living in Jerusalem as much as possible, the city was still the center for most of the day-to-day administration of the country and the seat of the Sanhedrin. Further evidence of government activity in the city can be seen in the Byzantine era when a large number of churches were constructed under official patronage and Jerusalem became once more the religious center of an empire, although not a temporal capital. Several ecclesiastical dignitaries lived in Jerusalem at this time, and it became a rather important center of church administraton. After the Arab conquest, Jerusalem became only a small provincial capital and the metropolis of Judea, and it was never raised to the status of an imperial center despite its sacred character to Moslems. Only during the Crusader period did the governmental function ever become strong again, when the city was very much a military stronghold and capital of the Latin Kingdom. After the 1914-18 War, Jerusalem became again the capital of the whole of Western Palestine under the British Mandate and the State of Israel made their part of the city its capital. Consequently, governmental activity is important again and much is now spent on roads and other social services in the city and the government building program is also large.

V

THE HOLY CITY

From what has been said already concerning the economic life of Jerusalem, the importance of the tourist industry can be clearly seen. In fact it is so essential to the city's existence that a separate treatment is necessary in order to deal fully with the nature and influence of the pilgrim and tourist trade. As an influence on the growth of early cities, religion has a very important place, as Lewis Mumford has pointed out. In Jerusalem perhaps more than other places we can see the action of the sacred as it impinges on the secular in an urban environment.

The idea of a sanctuary or holy site is very old; it also seems to have been universal. In the earliest cities of Mesopotamia were found large temples and sanctuaries, and it is logical to assume that smaller communities also had similar if less imposing edifices. The Old Testament contains frequent references to the high places and groves of ancient Canaan, whose naturalistic religions found expression in hilltops and woods. Even in the civilizations of Central America, the same phenomenon of temples and religious shrines can be found. As religious systems evolved and became more organized, one or two sites became more important and grew into major religious centers served by a resident priesthood and perhaps a sacred kingship. This function of a religious center became a very important one and such centers attracted large numbers of pilgrims and often they became commercial and administrative capitals as well.

The Jewish religion after the Exodus had a purity of faith and vision which distinguished it from the heathen religions of the Canaanites, but it also had a strong belief in the sanctity of certain places, especially those where the tombs of their ancestors were, or where the Ark of the Covenant rested. However, the prime sanctity was the land itself, Eretz Israel, the Holy Land which Jehovah had promised to them as their inheritance. Apart from this, Judaism has not encouraged the proliferation of sacred spots. There are fewer shrines and places of pilgrimage in Judaism than in Christianity or Islam and little of the mythology which has accompanied some of the traditional Christian holy places. Apart from Mt. Gerizim which became the Samaritan center, Judaism has had only two holy cities, Shiloh and Jerusalem. The former was the first cultic center after the settlement of the land, because there the Ark was kept, and it remained a witness to the scattered tribes of their essential unity in the Covenant with God. However, after the selection of Jerusalem as the city of David and the site for the Temple, and the destruction of Shiloh and removal of the Ark by the Philistines, only Jerusalem was recognized as the holy city of the Jewish faith. Even the associations of Tiberias or Safed were not strong enough in 1948 for the leaders of the new State of Israel to resist making Jerusalem the capital despite the fact that this defied all logic.

At first it was probably just the Temple which was sacred, but eventually the whole city became the theocratic as well as the political center of Israel. Jerusalem became in a way the symbol of the nation and the goal of men's aspirations. The psalms in particular record much of the feeling for "my holy hill of Zion" (Ps. 2:6). To the Israelites, Jerusalem was protected by God in a special way not applicable elsewhere:

> God is in the midst of her; she shall not be moved.
>
> —Ps. 46:4

and again:

> Strengthen O God that which thou hast wrought for us
> Because of thy temple at Jerusalem. — Ps. 68:28

or in the simple statement:

> The Lord doth build up Jerusalem. — Ps. 147:2

The whole city as well as the temple became the sacred place and center of worship for Jerusalem was the city of God and the Temple was His house. In Psalm 122, we have a hymn of a pilgrim which illustrates clearly what Jerusalem meant to the nation:

I was glad when they said unto me,
Let us go unto the house of the Lord.
Our feet are standing
Within thy gates, O Jerusalem;
Jerusalem, that art builded
As a city that is compact together:
Whither the tribes go up, even the tribes of the Lord,
For a testimony unto Israel,
To give thanks unto the name of the Lord.
For there are set thrones for judgement
The thrones of the house of David.
Pray for the peace of Jerusalem:
They shall prosper that love thee.
Peace be within thy walls,
And prosperity within thy palaces.
For my brethren and companions sakes,
I will now say, Peace be within thee.
For the sake of the house of the Lord our God
I will seek thy good.

So Jerusalem became the center of worship (verse 4) and became the national symbol. This growth can also be seen in a verse from Isaiah, where the prophet first refers to Zion hill where the Temple stood, and then to the whole city, and finally to the nation:

O thou that tellest good tidings to Zion, get thee up into the high mountains; O thou that tellest good tidings to Jerusalem, lift up thy voice with strength; lift it up, be not afraid; say unto the cities of Judah, Behold your God.
— Isa. 40:9

All this confidence in the holy city stands in marked contrast with the plaintive poetry of the Exiles.

If I forget thee, O Jerusalem,
Let my right hand forget her cunning. . . . — Ps. 137:5

Nevertheless, Jerusalem to the Jews could never be replaced, whether they were in exile in Babylon or in the U.S.A. During the second period of Jewish occupation of Palestine, at the time of Christ, pilgrimages were again in full swing and it became the object and goal of every true Jew to visit Jerusalem at least once in a lifetime. Its significance was such that Jesus saw that it was necessary for him to suffer and die *in Jerusalem* (Matt. 16:21). Even after their final expulsion from the city in the second century, the Jews always held a special affection for

Jerusalem and in the Middle Ages many older Jews were inspired with the idea of being buried at Jerusalem. It was inevitable, despite the alternatives, that the Zionists of the nineteenth and twentieth centuries should set their hearts on the sacred soil of Palestine and their holy city. Thus even the development of the Jerusalem of today can be regarded as due in large measure to the tenets of the Jewish religion and its love for its holy city.

Much of the feeling of Judaism for Jerusalem has rubbed off onto Christianity. With the Old Testament an integral part of the Christian Scriptures and the large amount of the New Testament which is set in the Jerusalem area, it is only natural that Christians should love the place where the world's redemption was wrought. Yet one of the first things which the early Church did was to jettison any idea of the sanctity of earthly sanc-

JERUSALEM TEMPLE AREA. Southwestern part, near the Gate of the Chain. Courtesy, Levant Photo Service

tuaries or objects. The Jewish Christians appear to have continued to worship in the Temple, but Jesus had already prophesied its downfall and the Church meetings seem to have taken place in ordinary private houses rather than special buildings set apart. The Christian regarded himself as the "temple of God" (I Cor. 3:16), and there was a concept of the new Jerusalem in heaven (Rev. 21:2), but the earthly city was not held particularly sacred. Yet in contrast to this, today we find that Christianity has more holy sites scattered throughout the world than any other monotheistic religion, and none is more sacred than Jerusalem and the sanctuaries there. Despite competition, especially in times when travel was difficult, from Rome or Canterbury, Jerusalem has continued to be the object of Christian pilgrims as it was to the Jew of old. There have been two motives for Christian pilgrimages:

1) To gain forgiveness for sin. This particularly applied to Roman Catholics, after the advent of indulgences. In the Middle Ages, a Roman Catholic could sin for a lifetime and gain ample remission in a week at Jerusalem, so many were sent there on penance.

2) To gain instruction in the Scriptures and learn more about the place where Jesus taught and died and where Solomon ruled in such splendor. This has been the predominant motive of Protestant visitors.

It is important to bear these motives in mind, because they have influenced the number and the location of religious shrines in the city. Thus the indulgence system has undoubtedly influenced the multiplicity of Roman Catholic holy places, although this community has often been small in numbers. The Greek and Armenian Christians have tended to concentrate their efforts on the Holy Sepulcher Church and have crowded into the Old City. The Protestants, with less concern for authentic Scriptural locations, have tended to build Churches and hospices wherever land is available, even outside the Old City and have fostered the growth of the Garden Tomb, not on the grounds of authenticity, but because it is more realistic than the Holy Sepulcher.

In Islam, holy place and pilgrimage are very real concepts and the latter is one of the pillars of the faith. It is, however, to Mecca that the Moslem turns to pray and goes on the pilgrimage, and although Jerusalem is important as a holy city (hence its Arab name of Al Kuds), it cannot replace Mecca. Attempts to make Jerusalem the object of the pilgrimage instead of Mecca, by Abd al Malik, never succeeded. Nevertheless, Jerusalem is an important holy city to the Moslem. It was the scene of Mohammed's night journey and Islamic belief holds — along with traditional Judaism and Christianity — that the Last Judgment will take place in the Kidron Valley. For a Moslem unable or unwilling to take the long trip to Mecca, Jerusalem is a good substitute, as it is accessible to most parts of the Islamic Middle East. It has often been a stopping place en route to Mecca for pilgrims from Turkey, Iran and Syria, although the occupation of the city by Israel may now stop this trade. To the Moslem, the sacred place in Jerusalem is the Haram enclosure which includes the Dome of the Rock and the Al Aqsa mosque, although there are a number of old mosques of some fame in the city. Jewish devotions in the city have similarly been centered around the Haram, in their case the stretch of Herodian walling generally known as the "Wailing Wall," although there are also a number of tombs in the vicinity which are visited. Christianity has a much greater spread of holy sites, for although the Holy Sepulcher is probably the most popular place, it is fast losing preeminence to the Garden Tomb and such sites as the Sisters of Zion convent and the Pool of Bethesda, with their visible remains of the past. They are visited by practically all pilgrims. In addition there are several holy places on the Mount of Olives and in the Garden of Gethsemane which are very popular. This is one of the reasons why Christian pilgrimages are more important for a study of the geography of Jerusalem than are those of Judaism or Islam — the spread of holy sites has brought about a far greater impact on the urban scene and effected urban distributions.

THE DEVELOPMENT OF THE PILGRIM/TOURIST TRADE

As we have seen, the development of holy places occurred very early in man's history and with them came the development of the pilgrimage. Melchizedek, one of the pre-Israelite kings of Jerusalem seems to have been a priest-king and so the city may even at that early date have been a pilgrimage center. Indeed, it has been suggested that Abraham's visit to Mount Moriah was a type of pilgrimage. Jerusalem seems to have taken over as a place for the worship of Jehovah even before the building of the Temple, for there was a place of worship on the Mount of Olives during the reign of David (II Sam. 15:32). After the building of the Temple, pilgrimage seems to have been a regular part of the Jewish religious experience. In

DOME OF THE ASCENSION (QUBBAT AL MI'RAJ). This small qubba in the Temple Area is the traditional site of Mohammed's ascent to heaven.

Psalm 84 we have a song of a pilgrim who has wended his way through the "valley of Weeping" (i.e. the upper part of the Wadi Shilo, the valley of the Robbers), and finds it all worthwhile, for

> . . . a day in thy courts is better than a thousand.
> I had rather be a doorkeeper in the house of my God,
> Than to dwell in the tents of wickedness. — Ps. 84:10

After the return from Exile, and especially during the Pax Romana, pilgrimages were frequent. On the occasion of the birth of the first male, it was apparently customary to visit Jerusalem (Luke 2:23) and during the Passover, the city was normally crowded (Luke 22:1). Josephus estimated 2,000,000 in the city on one occasion, and although he no doubt exaggerated, the impression must have been that of a full city. Many private pilgrimages must have been made (Acts 21), so that, as at present, there were periods of peak crowding in the city, followed by a steady flow of off-peak visitors.[1]

Jewish pilgrimages were interrupted in A.D. 70 and stopped completely after the founding of Aelia Capitolina in A.D. 132. When Christians first began to go on pilgrimages is a much discussed point. There is no evidence in the New Testament that it was a usual practice for the early Christians, and there is no record of a pilgrimage until the account of the Bordeaux Pilgrim in the fourth century. He was no doubt not the first, but it still seems that there was a complete break in pilgrim activity in Jerusalem for the second and third centuries A.D. The next boom period did not come until the Byzantine period and the activities of Helena in the vicinity of the city. This queen founded many churches, and hospices were also built. The Empress Eudoxia was also responsible for the construction of buildings and the pilgrim industry began to revive not only for Christians but also for Jews, for the Bordeaux Pilgrim records that they had a "wailing place," presumably the present Wailing Wall. In all, it seems from contemporary accounts that there were large numbers of pilgrims each year in Jerusalem from all over the civilized world of that time and by the sixth century it seems that many came to stay, for Antoninus Martyr records that there were a large number of hermits living on the Mount of Olives. There was a considerable pilgrim traffic along the Via Maris coast road and the inhabitants of Gaza were described

---

1 For Jewish pilgrimages and especially comments on the pilgrim psalms, see J. Schreiner, *Sion-Jerusalem Jahwes Konigsitz* (1963).

by one writer as "lovers of pilgrims." The effect on Jerusalem can be seen in the large number of churches which were erected at that time. By the early part of the sixth century there were twenty-four churches on the Mount of Olives and a large number within the walled city. Jerusalem never looked back after this early boom in the pilgrim trade and even the Moslem conquest of the city could not dispel the travelers who made their way from Europe and the other parts of the Middle East to see the holy city. The introduction of Islam into Jerusalem brought in the third religious element, for by the time of the visit of Arculfus in 680, there was a Moslem place of prayer over the Sakhra rock, visited by many pilgrims. Jerusalem never attracted quite the crowds of pilgrims which Mecca was able to do, but according to Nasir-i-Khusrau it was considered an alternative for those unable to face the long journey through the desert. Many passed through the city on the way to Mecca, and in some years there were apparently as many as 20,000 in Jerusalem on the first day of the pilgrimage. Also, large numbers retired to the city in old age to await the resurrection. Large numbers of Christians continued to visit Jerusalem as there was considerable toleration of minorities and the great festivals attracted large crowds to the Holy Sepulcher which could hold, by contemporary estimates, 8,000 pilgrims and was frequently full. A large number of the pilgrims came from Western Europe, i.e. the Roman Catholic or Latin Church, but the dominant groups at this time seem to have been the Eastern Churches who had the ease of access, living in relative proximity to the city and able to travel more freely within the Arab empires. However some interruption of the pilgrim journeys after the invasion of the Seljuk Turks brought about difficulties for the pilgrims. Inspired by the fanatic preaching of Peter the Hermit, many Christian kings of the West were induced to undertake the invasions of Palestine which we call the Crusades. The Crusading period brought about the dominance of the Latin Church on the ecclesiastical scene in the Holy Land and the Eastern churches — to which the native Christians belonged — found the so-called Christian kingdoms a mixed blessing. Anyhow, it certainly brought about a new revival of pilgrimages from Western Europe and a new spate in the construction of churches and the location of holy places. The Haram area was taken over and made into a church and the headquarters of the Knights Templar. Hospices were also built to accommodate this new surge of pilgrims and certain convents and religious orders became quite wealthy. The whole valley of the Kidron belonged to the Con-

THE VIRGIN'S TOMB in Gethsemane.

vent of the Virgin's Tomb, which was one of the most popular holy sites. The population of the city expanded, partly by the increase in clerics and also because a number of pilgrims, unable to afford the fare back home, were forced to stay and work in the land. Their descendants can often be seen today, distinguished by fair hair and skin and other European traits, particularly in the Bethlehem area.

After the Crusader period, there was a slight decline in pilgrim visitation to Jerusalem, but once it was realized that the Moslems were not going to return the outrages perpetrated on them by the conquering Crusaders, the traffic returned in force. We have an interesting account of the city in the early thirteenth century, written by an unknown author and entitled *Citez de Jherusalem,* to which reference has already been made. From this we learn that there were still many monks in the city and hospices for pilgrims. We learn, too, that the "Saracens" had started to charge pilgrims for entry to the Holy Sepulcher. This practice was to continue until recent times and was a fruitful source of income to the family who held the right of entry. It later caused the Pope to forbid pilgrimages to Jerusalem for fear of strengthening the Moslems by making them rich on the pilgrim trade, although it seems that the ban had little effect. Later in the thirteenth century, Moslem dominance seems to have brought about a decline in both the Christian population of Jerusalem and also in the pilgrimages, but the rise of the indulgence system revived the trade. Niccolo of Poggibonsi even compiled a list of the indulgences to be gained by a trip to Jerusalem. By the end of the fifteenth century there were at least enough pilgrims visiting the city each year for a warning to be issued forbidding visitors to carve their names and coat of arms on masonry in the city! There were a number of hospices for Latin and Greek (i.e. Arab members of the Greek Orthodox Church) pilgrims. The guardianship of the holy places by the Franciscans helped considerably in the later Middle Ages to place the pilgrimage industry on a secure footing, and the businesslike efforts of Suriano and Bernadino Amico gave the pilgrim activities of the time an appearance not unlike that of the modern tourist industry. From the frequent complaints about shortage of lodgings in the city, despite the many monasteries and hospices there, it can be inferred that there was quite an increase in pilgrim numbers towards the end of the Middle Ages.

A decline set in after the conquest of Palestine by the Ottoman Turks, and the pilgrim trade thinned out considerably. There were many exactions and tolls, not only in the Holy Land but en route there, and the way was dangerous. Maundrell sums up the pilgrim's path:

> To accomplish the said journey, it is necessary to set aside all thoughts of relatives, wives, children, property, treasure, and of every kind of comfort which can be had in the homeland.

Yet it is not really just to blame the Turks completely for this decline in the pilgrim trade. Admittedly, they were often heavy handed in attempts to exact as much money as possible from the pilgrim but by the sixteenth century they were beginning to realize that the constant demands for "protection money" was so deterring pilgrims that they were losing more than they gained. Innumerable legends were concocted by the native Arabs of Jerusalem in order to get as much money as possible from those pilgrims who did manage to make it to the city. Many of the causes of the decline, however, were to be found elsewhere. The growth of the Protestant churches in Europe meant that now a large part of the population of the West — and its richest part — were no longer interested in pilgrimages, and the energies of the Roman Church were taken up with combating the new teachings. In addition, there seems to have been a growth of scepticism even among Roman Catholics regarding the authenticity of the holy sites, so the journey seemed less worthwhile. Maundrell records that there were some thousands of pilgrims in Jerusalem while he was there, but the bulk of visitors may well have been from the Eastern churches. Such was the lack of trade, that Madden records that even the monks competed to entertain visitors in their hospices. There seem to have been a number of Jewish pilgrims in the city, but Robinson noted that the Christian pilgrims at Easter were nearly all from the Greek or Armenian churches, and the Latin pilgrims were so few that they all managed to be accommodated in the Latin convent. So even in the early part of the nineteenth century, the pilgrim trade was at a pretty low ebb.

Since the explorations of the country and its accurate mapping in the second half of the last century, however, the number of pilgrims has increased until today more people than ever before converge on the city at Easter and Christmas. Increasing wealth in Western Europe and the increasing ease and safety of transport, have probably been the main factors in this development, for much of the increase has not come through religious pilgrimages of the old type, but has been through the growth of a modern tourist industry. The tremendous increase in the number of Protestants visiting the Holy Land has been of great significance, especially in the relative importance of the particular holy sites and the expenditure of the visitors on "souvenirs."[2] There has also been a great increase in the num-

---

2 State of Israel, Ministry of Tourism, *Survey of Tourism* (1966/67, In Hebrew).

ber of Jewish visitors, apart from those who came to settle. In particular during the Mandate period, a modern tourist industry began to develop in Palestine with the building of new roads, the improvement of accommodations and the publication of guide books. The number of visitors seeing Jerusalem each year was well over 300,000 before 1967 and may well go even higher if the political situation settles. However, 1967 and 1968 have been poor years for visits of Christian pilgrims and tourists, for despite the advantages of a "united" city, the prospect of war and civil disturbance has discouraged many people. This is ample illustration of how irregular the pilgrim/tourist trade in Jerusalem is, for events of international significance — war or a slump — can make a boom year to be followed by a poor year and affluence to be succeeded by poverty. Hence the need to make Jerusalem much less dependent on the tourist trade and to develop light industry and other trades to offset the irregularity in the flow of overseas visitors.

PILGRIM ITINERARIES

An important feature of the pilgrim/tourist industry is where the visitors go when they get to Jerusalem, because distribution of tourist activity vitally effects the spacial growth of the city and is of considerable importance in attempting to plan the location of green belts, residential areas, and hotels, etc. Anyone who has tried to walk down the Suq Khan es-Zeit against the flow of a religious procession while being prodded in the back by a barrow boy, will realize that this is not just an academic question, but a matter of great practical importance.

To the Jew there is only one building of real importance — the Temple. It was in the Temple that the sacrifices were made in ancient times and it was the Temple which symbolized more than anything else the presence of God in His Holy City. It was in the Temple that Jesus was "presented," and it was to the Temple that He and His disciples first went on the entry to the city just before His death. Other places are of interest to Jews, in particular the Tomb of David in its traditional spot on Mt. Zion, and there are many tombs in the Jerusalem area which are sacred to those of the Jewish faith. Yet there is really no substitute for the Temple, and so even today, the many Jewish tombs are visited by few people, but vast crowds congregate on the Sabbath at the Wailing Wall. This stretch of wall is part of the Temple of Herod and seems to have been used by Jews as a substitute for the Temple since at least the fourth century. As we have seen, the Bordeaux pilgrim saw them worship at a "perforated stone" where they would "bewail themselves with groans, rend their garments and so depart." The first action of the Jewish army on entering the city in June, 1967, was to worship at the Wailing Wall, where for obvious security reasons, they had been unable to go since 1948. Apart from the tombs of various prophets and the haram at Hebron, the main Jewish holy places apart from the Wailing Wall are the Tomb of Rachel, on the road to Bethlehem and the Shrine of the Book, a recent construction which is quite popular as a quasi-religious monument.

The Moslem pattern of pilgrim visitation is similar to that of the Jews, i.e. an intense concentration on the Temple area, with a lesser veneration for a selection of tombs and ancient mosques. As the scene of Mohammed's night journey and ascent into heaven, the Haram is of considerable importance and a key holy site in Islam. Inside the enclosure, the chief points of pilgrim interest are the Dome of the Rock, which in its present form dates back to 691, when it was built under the instructions of the Ommayad Khalif, Abd el-Malik bin Marwan, with tiles added by Suleiman the Magnificent in 1561. It covers the

THE WAILING WALL. This is part of the western wall of the Haram enclosure and includes stretches of the masonry erected by Herod the Great. The open space in front of the wall was occupied by private houses before the war in 1967.

rock which is probably the site of the altar of sacrifice in the
Jewish Temple, but it is not a real mosque, for the mosque in
the Haram area is the Al-Aqsa mosque south of the Dome of
the Rock, which was first built in 709 and frequently rebuilt and
repaired. Just outside the Holy Sepulcher Church is another
ancient Moslem building, the Mosque of Omar, which was built
in 1216 by Shehab ed-Din on the spot where the Khalif Omar
prayed after entering the city in 636 A.D.

In contrast to the intense concentration of the Jewish and
Moslem pilgrims on just a few holy places, the Christian pilgrim has an itinerary which includes something in practically
every corner of the city. The table below gives some idea of
the number of Christian holy places and the frequency of
visits to them. It will be seen that the Church of the Holy
Sepulcher is visited by all parties, but that there are a number
of other sites which are just as popular, including the Haram
enclosure, the Garden of Gethsemane and Bethany. At Easter,
the Holy Sepulcher is usually full and the center of attraction,
but in normal times many visitors prefer the quieter places outside the Old City — the Garden of Gethsemane, the Mount of
Olives and the Garden Tomb to mention a few. Those sites
which have good remains of the ancient city visible are popular,
especially the Sisters of Zion Convent with its Roman pave-
ment and St. Peter in Gallicantu, with an ancient dungeon among
its attractions. Most of the sites are open, i.e. visitors can walk
in freely, but some are closed and visitors are shown around
by a guide. The main ones in this category are in fact those
with ancient remains visible, including the Russian Excavations
as well as the two just mentioned. Today, there are only a few
holy sites at which payment has to be made, namely the Haram
area, the Church of the Ascension (now a mosque) and the
Russian Church on Gethsemane, but in former times many
more sites charged for admission and a pilgrim could run up a
large expense sheet.

Within the Old City, the best known site is the Holy Sepulcher.
Its authenticity has been a much debated point and at the present time there is still no evidence that this is the actual tomb
of Christ. Good arguments have been put forward to show that
this is probably the most likely area, but they are not completely
convincing and the general appearance of the church has not
impressed visitors, so that many have preferred the "rival"
claimant, the Garden Tomb. Much of the argument centers
around whether or not the Christians of the first and second
centuries A.D. preserved a knowledge of the places where Christ

was crucified and buried, for we have no evidence of there being any building of a Christian nature on this spot prior to the construction of Constantine's basilica. No evidence in the New Testament or the earliest Christian writings is forthcoming to show that these spots were venerated. Consequently, the history of the Holy Sepulcher begins with Constantine, or rather with his mother, Helena, whose activities in the city have already been mentioned. She found what was supposed to be the true cross just east of the present sepulcher. This act is commemorated in the Chapel of St. Helena and the Grotto of the Finding of the Holy Cross, which are part of the Holy Sepulcher building. A church was built which survived until the Persians destroyed it and many other churches in their capture of Jerusalem in 614, but it was quickly rebuilt in 628 by Modestus. Omar nobly refrained from praying within the church when he entered the city in 636, and so prevented Moslems staking any claim to it, but the Church has still been riven as much by the feuds between Greek, Latin, Armenian and Copt as it has by the numerous earthquakes which have from time to time damaged the structure. Extensive work was done on the church by the Crusaders and the many separate chapels incorporated under one roof, but little else has been done until recent years when extensive restorations have been in progress.

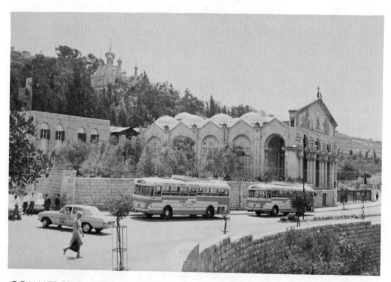

COMMERCIAL GETHSEMANE (1). Buses and taxis have brought tourists to the Church of All Nations (foreground) and the Russian Church.

The church is now open and free, but until 1832 payment was necessary to get in, the fee being five to six ducats in the Middle Ages. Pilgrims were then locked in over the Easter weekend, and food and provisions were sold to them in a market which was held inside the church. The church is sacred to all branches of the Christian church, commemorating the place of crucifixion and burial and resurrection of Jesus. Copts and Syrians have preciously guarded rights there as well as the larger bodies.

Near the Holy Sepulcher, on the northeast corner of the

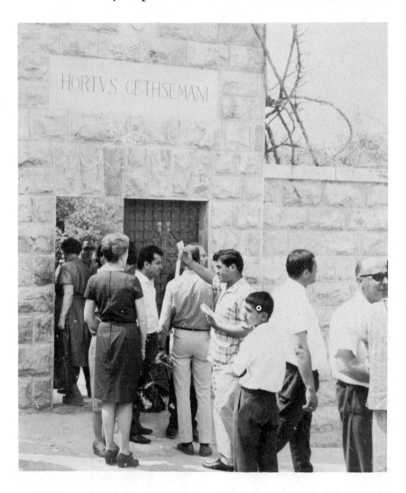

COMMERCIAL GETHSEMANE (2). Vendors ply a lively trade outside the garden entrance.

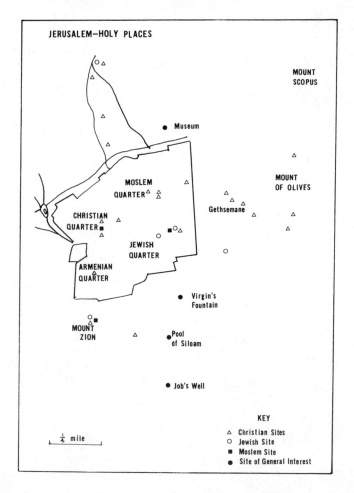

JERUSALEM—HOLY PLACES

MOUNT SCOPUS

● Museum

MOSLEM QUARTER

MOUNT OF OLIVES

Gethsemane

CHRISTIAN QUARTER

JEWISH QUARTER

ARMENIAN QUARTER

Virgin's Fountain

MOUNT ZION

●Pool of Siloam

● Job's Well

KEY

△ Christian Sites
○ Jewish Site
■ Moslem Site
● Site of General Interest

¼ mile

Muristan is the Church of the Redeemer, a Lutheran church built in 1898 on the site of a Crusader church which was dedicated to St. Mary Latina Major, with ownership retained by the Knights of St. John of Jerusalem. It is popular with Lutherans, and large numbers climb its tower to see the magnificent view of the Old City.

Within the Old City itself, the area with the most Christian holy sites is the northeastern part of the Moslem Quarter, just north of the Haram, along the Via Dolorosa. Here are found the sites connected with the judgment and scourging of Christ. They have flourished largely because of the remains still visible. The Sisters of Zion convent is visited by most parties of pilgrims staying more than just a few days; so is the Flagellation Convent which is next door. The present buildings here are relatively modern (acquired in the nineteenth century) but in Crusader times there were three chapels in this area, so its importance is not new. However, the sites were not operating in later Arab and Ottoman times. On the southern side of the Via Dolorosa lies a school built over part of the citadel which existed here in New Testament times to dominate the Temple and which is a likely site for the judgment of Christ. Hence, the weekly Stations of the Cross procession begins here. Just inside the St. Stephen's Gate, is the St. Anne's Church and seminary. The traditional Pool of Bethesda, which is here, has been mentioned already, but there is an ancient tradition that this is the site of the house where the Virgin Mary was born, and so it has additional importance for Roman Catholics. Other Christian sites of importance in the Old City include the Russian Excavations, some old walls now enclosed in a building, the Armenian Ca-

GORDON'S CALVARY, from the grounds of the Garden Tomb.

thedral of St. James with its fine murals and the Syrian Orthodox Cathedral which is in the northeast corner of the Armenian Quarter. These last two places are of considerable importance to the native pilgrims, whose numbers are larger than most Western visitors realize. In addition most Christian pilgrims visit the Haram enclosure and the Wailing Wall and wander down the suqs to buy souvenirs.

To the north of the Old City there are only two holy sites of importance. The Garden Tomb lies just north of the bus station and east of the Nablus Road. It extends beneath a rocky hill which has been quarried in the past, and is generally known in the west as "Gordon's Calvary" because of the beliefs of that famous general. The Garden Tomb has become very popular since then, in part as a Protestant reaction against the Holy Sepulcher and in part because it is a much more pleasant site and gives a much better idea of what an ancient tomb was like. It is too far north of the city wall of the first century A.D. to be authentic, but is steadily growing in favor with visitors from America and Europe. Further to the north, near the junction of Saladin Street and the Nablus Road are the Tombs of the Kings, owned by the French government and quite popular with visitors of all denominations, including now large numbers of Jews. They in fact date not from the times of the Jewish kings but from the first century A.D., and are probably the tombs of Queen Helena of Adiabene and her family, who were converts to Judaism and natives of Mesopotamia.

South of the Old City are a number of sites on the itineraries of most pilgrims. The Pool of Siloam has been a popular site for visitors for many centuries and particularly in Byzantine times. On the traditional Mount Zion lie a number of buildings which are holy to Christian pilgrims, of which St. Peter in Gallicantu is one of the most popular. It stands on one of the suggested sites for the house of Caiaphas and has some very excellent remains. Its fame is, however, relatively recent since the present church was built by the Assumptionist Fathers, but there is evidence that it was venerated in Byzantine times and is probably the site of the Crusader Church of St. Peter. Further up the hill is a group of buildings of very ancient origin, which include the Tomb of David, under Jewish control, the Coenaculum or room of the Last Supper, the Dormition Abbey, where Mary is supposed to have died, and another claimant for Caiaphas' house. These sites were, until 1967, the only ones around the Old City which were accessible from Israel, and had relatively few visitors, but in the Middle Ages this was the site of the Latin hospice and official headquarters. All three are mentioned in pilgrim accounts of Byzantine and Mediaeval date.

The final group of Christian holy sites is on the Mount of Olives or in its vicinity. This area is very popular with pilgrims today, as it has been over the centuries, mainly because of the magnificent views of Jerusalem and the Wilderness of Judea which can be obtained from the summit. The place of the Ascension on the top of the hill is a very ancient place of veneration for Christians, although often not visited today. Further down the hill are the newer buildings of Dominus Flevit, built in 1955 over fifth-century remains, and the Russian Church which dates from the last century. The Ascension place was first built on in the fourth century, and it remained one of the most popular pilgrim places until 1187 when the Moslems took it over. Near this place is the Church of Pater Noster, which is modern in its present building, but is on the site of the first church built on the Mount of Olives, called Eleona (olive grove) and built in 330 by Helena. At the foot of the Mount is the Garden of Gethsemane, which has always been popular with pilgrims, and the Basilica of the Agony (also called the Church of All Nations), a church with fourth-century origins, but rebuilt by the Crusaders. The present building was erected in the present century by the Franciscans, and is one of the most fre-

MOUNT OF OLIVES. A Palm Sunday procession ascends the eastern side of the Mount.

quented holy sites. Near by is another old site, the Tomb of the
Virgin, which was turned into a church in the fifth century. At
one time it was as popular with pilgrims as the Holy Sepulcher
is now, particularly in the Middle Ages. It has had a turbu-
lent ownership, and although for many years under Roman
Catholic control, in 1757 the Turkish authorities gave it to the
Eastern churches, who now have joint control.

So it can be seen that the distribution of holy sites is not even,
but is concentrated in clusters especially around the center
of the Old City, the northeast, the Mount of Olives and Mount
Zion. Roman Catholic sites have the widest spread, especially
as that church has been active in the last century or so in re-
constructing old sites and building fine new churches on them.
In fact all the sites on the Mount of Olives, except the mosque
at the place of Ascension and the Tomb of the Virgin, have had
relatively recent buildings constructed on them. This indicates
the general sparsity of sites in the city which date back to the
later Arab and Ottoman times. To judge by the remains, in Byzantine and Crusader times there were many more sites than today, yet over half of the present churches visited by pilgrims are
of recent construction. The native churches concentrate their
pilgrim activity inside the Old City and seem to attach greater
importance to the Holy Sepulcher than do the Western churches.
Roman Catholic sites being strongest along the Via Dolorosa and
the Mount of Olives area, it is not surprising that the route from
Gethsemane to the Via Dolorosa via St. Stephen's Gate and then
to the Holy Sepulcher via the Suq Khan es-Zeit, is the busiest
of the pilgrim routes.

VI

THE POPULATION AND AREA

One of the most difficult tasks which the geographer faces in analyzing an urban community is to estimate its size particularly in past centuries. Censuses were taken as far back as the Bronze Age (Num. 1) but few records were kept and we have no idea how accurate these early enumerations were. Although the geographer is primarily concerned with the area on the ground rather than the size of population as such, the two are obviously closely linked, and so discussion of the acreage covered by a city is tied in with the problems of determining its population. Apart from the problem of lack of numerical data, there are also problems of lack of knowledge of the density of population within the city and of the actual area of residential housing as opposed to public buildings. Thus simply to take the area enclosed by the walls — even where these are known — and to estimate from that the population of the city, is not a reliable practice. Nor can the area be determined from the number of inhabitants. There might well be extra-mural settlements in times of peace which confuse the problem, as well as empty spaces within the walls at other times.

ANCIENT JERUSALEM

For Jerusalem, there are certain estimates of population from the time of the return from the Exile which can be used to determine the number of the inhabitants of the city and help to estimate the area within the walls. The earliest and most detailed is that in Nehemiah 7. Here it is recorded that "the city was wide and large; but the people were few therein, and the houses were not builded" (Neh. 7:4), which illustrates that area and population size do not necessarily go together. The

result was a census of the returned Jews and eventually a decision was reached to allow one in ten to dwell in Jerusalem; the
rest settled elsewhere. The figures given are 42,360 returning
Jews with 7,337 servants and 245 singers, giving a total population for the small province of Judah (ignoring any native inhabitants) as 49,942. Of these, the figures for the population of Jerusalem (Neh. 11) are: 468 of the tribe of Judah; 928 of Benjamin;
1192 priests; 284 Levites and 172 gatewatchers, i.e. 3,044 in total. To these we might add 10 per cent of the servants, i.e.
730, and all the singers, 245, giving a total male population of
4,000 or so, and a similar number of women. Considering Lewis
Mumford's estimate of 5,000 as the normal population of the
average ancient city, this figure is probably correct and can be
regarded as the most accurate and detailed early census ex-
tant. Nehemiah's dismay at the low numbers must be seen in
relation to the size of Jerusalem just before the Exile. No doubt
there was much green grass within the walls for some time
after the return.

Other evidence for the size of the Old Testament city can be
obtained from areal studies, but involved here is a great deal
of uncertainty, as there is little positive evidence for the course
of the walls of the city until post-Biblical times, and there has
been considerable controversy over the exact position of the
ancient walls.[1] However, using both literary sources and archaeological evidence, the area of the ancient city is gradually being
revealed, and more assurance can be obtained on the subject
than was possible half a century ago.

The size of the city of David and Solomon, and the old Jebusite city before it, is tied up with its location. The traditional
site of Zion on the broad southwestern hill was held by most
people as the location of the city until the beginning of this
century when George Adam Smith began advocating the location of "David's Burgh" on the southeastern hill or Ophel. The
difference in size between the two hills is enormous and it is the
small size of Ophel which caused many scholars to reject it as
the site of ancient Jerusalem. However, while the fourteen acres
which make up that hill may seem puny compared with the
240 acres of Carchemish, 600 acres of Mohenjo-Daro and 1800
acres of Nineveh, in relation to other Palestinian sites it is large.
A location on the Ophel hill was also dismissed by Claude Conder and other military men on the grounds of inadequate
defense, but its steep sides would rather help defense and the

---

1 G. A. Smith, *Jerusalem*, Vol. I, Ch. 8.

54 acres of the southwestern hill would have certainly been largely empty in the days when the city's population was only a few thousand. Further complications in assessing the size of early Jerusalem came with the suggestions of certain scholars that there were in fact two cities, Zion and the City of David, one on the western hill and the other on Ophel. A recent paper by the late Pierce Hubbard has suggested that originally there were two cities, Urusalim on the southwest hill and Jebus on the Ophel hill.[2] Needless to say this would be a most unusual urban community and the theories are as yet unproven. No excavation, including the recent campaigns of Kathleen Kenyon, have unearthed evidence of early occupation of the southwest hill, whereas we now have a good picture of the walls and some of the structures of the early city on Ophel. The eastern wall is

2 P. Hubbard, *P.E.Q.* (1966).

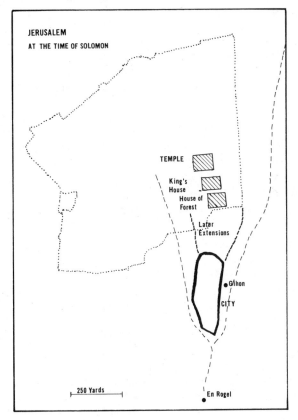

JERUSALEM
AT THE TIME OF SOLOMON

TEMPLE

King's
House

House of
Forest

Later
Extensions

Gihon

CITY

250 Yards

En Rogel

now clearly traceable, and with the spring of Gihon nearby, it seems certain that this hill was the site of the early cities of the Jebusites and of David. What population it carried would depend on the amount of land taken up with public buildings and streets, but in ancient times people seem generally to have been able to live in more crowded quarters than today. Allowing fifty square feet per person, which is common in modern Oriental towns, and an actual residential area of about ten acres, that would mean a population on the Ophel hill of about 3,000 for the City of David.

If one assumes a basic population of about 3,000, then difficulties still arise in assessing the growth of the city during the times of the later kings. Solomon's building projects and encouragement of trade must have brought about a considerable increase in population and in the built-up area. If Kathleen Kenyon is right and the "Millo" which David and Solomon built (II Sam. 5:9; I Kings 9:15) is really the terraces which expanded the southeast hill and were dug through by the recent excavations, then this could represent an early realization of the cramped nature of the site and an attempt to absorb a population increase without expanding outside the easily defendable Ophel ridge. It is likely, however, that there had been some building to the north, around the Temple and along the roads which entered the city from the north and west, for this is the direction from which came most of the trade. With the activities surrounding the Temple, an expansion of residential quarters into and up the Tyropoeon valley seems quite likely — in times of peace, anyway.

Many scholars have held out for the inclusion of the southwest hill into Jerusalem sometime after the reign of Solomon, the main reasons being:

1) This is a good site for residential expansion, being more easily defended and more pleasant than the Tyropoeon, which would have been left open.

2) The tunnel built by Hezekiah from Gihon to the Pool of Siloam would only make sense if the latter were within the city walls. This would suggest, especially in view of the findings of Bliss and Dickie, that the southwest hill was included at that time.

3) The account of Nehemiah's activites implies (though it does not state) that his wall building was on the lines of the pre-Exilic walls, and to judge by the number of gates and their

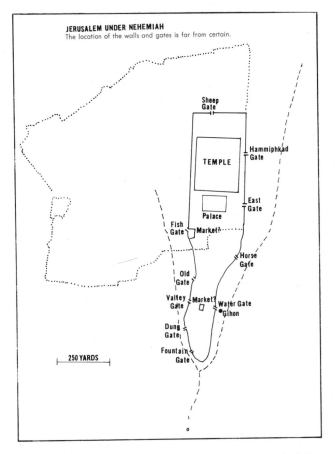

JERUSALEM UNDER NEHEMIAH
The location of the walls and gates is far from certain.

Sheep Gate

TEMPLE

Hammiphkad Gate

East Gate

Palace

Fish Gate

Market?

Horse Gate

Old Gate

Valley Gate

Market?

Water Gate

Gihon

Dung Gate

Fountain Gate

250 YARDS

names, would suggest a circuit which included both hills. This was amply argued by George Adam Smith and Pere Vincent and more recently by Simons. However, the excavations of Dr. Kenyon have revealed that the wall of Nehemiah on the east followed the line of the crest of Ophel, but no remains were found on the southwest hill south of the present walls. There is some evidence that there was expansion to the north, influenced by the main trade routes and the presence of the Temple. Certainly after Nehemiah's time there was an expansion of population west of the Temple area until a new wall had to be built. In general, though, it seems that Nehemiah's Jerusalem was about the same size within the walls, as that of Solomon, but with some adjustment of the actual line of the defenses, with a retreat of the eastern wall onto the summit of the Ophel ridge and a slight extension to the west into the Tyropoeon valley.

There certainly seems to have been expansion in the Hellenistic and Roman eras, the city beginning to take over a considerable area to the north, although there is no positive evidence of a general occupation of the southwest hill before the time of Herod Agrippa. For the actual area of the city in classical times, we rely very heavily upon the accounts of Josephus, the Jewish historian-soldier, whose report of the Roman capture of Jerusalem in A.D. 70 is invaluable. According to Josephus, there was a "first" wall which, it is generally agreed, ran round the southeast hill and included at least the northern part of the southwest hill. In the north, this wall ran from the Citadel (now erroneously known as the Tower of David), to the Xystus which lay due east of the tower, and then the wall ran to the western wall of the Temple. Older scholars drew the wall round the whole of the southwest hill to make the city roughly square in shape, but it now seems more likely that it was smaller than this, with a less regular shape. The areal size of Jerusalem in the immediate post-Exilic period, enclosed by the First Wall, would imply a population of about 12,000. However, Josephus does mention a "Second Wall" which enclosed extra-mural growth beyond the first northern wall and must have been constructed sometime in the Hellenistic/Hasmonaean period. Again the direction of the trading routes and the proximity of relatively flat ground for building would encourage growth in this direction, but it would also pose defensive problems, for there is no natural defense and a new wall must have become necessary. The course of this Second Wall and the area it enclosed has probably consumed more ink and paper in the controversy surrounding it than any comparable stretch of masonry, because its course vitally effects the authenticity of the Holy Sepulcher. This famous church cannot be authentic if it stands on a spot which was within the city walls at the time of Christ. There have been three main theories about the course of this wall: 1) A wide course which includes the Holy Sepulcher and, in many cases, is conjectured to extend as far north as the present north wall. This was the view of Robinson, Schick, and many of the British and American scholars of the last century, and if true would imply a very large population in this northern quarter at the beginning of the Christian era.[3] 2) A stepped course, excluding the Holy Sepulcher and leaving it within a bend in the wall. This has been advanced by Warren, Vincent, and Professor M. Avi-Yonah.[4]

---

3 Smith, *Jerusalem*, p. 247.

4 Prof. Avi-Yonah's latest expression of his views on the ancient topography of Jerusalem can be seen in his model of the city at the Holyland Hotel, Jerusalem.

3) A short course enclosing a small square which would cover part of the upper Tyropoeon. As this leaves the Holy Sepulcher right outside the city, this theory has been enthusiastically adopted by a number of Roman Catholic scholars, and there is much to be said in its favor, for certain evidence from the recent British excavations in the city point in this direction.[5] It does signify, however, that only a small area was built up outside the old north walls.

The problem of the course of this Second North Wall is a very tricky one, especially as Josephus' description is not very helpful. He simply describes the wall as running from "the Gennath Gate in the first wall and, enclosing only the northern quarter of the town, reached Antonia." Antonia we know as the fortress guarding the northern approaches to the Temple, but the location of the Gennath Gate is still uncertain. Jewish tombs have been found near the Holy Sepulcher and the recent excavations failed to find evidence of buildings of a Biblical date in the Muristan area, so a shorter course is now in favor, but the question of the size of this northern growth and the course of this wall is still not really settled. If the shorter course were adopted, this would give a city in New Testament times covering an area of about 97 acres with a population of about 30,000.

With the advantages of the Pax Romana and the policies of the Herods, there seems to have been an even larger expansion to the north in the first century A.D. With comparative wealth and freedom of movement enabling Jews to fulfil their pilgrimages and the efficient centralizing activities of the Jewish kings, the city expanded in population and no doubt in wealth also. There was the growth of a new suburb to the north called "Bezetha" and Herod Agrippa had to build yet another wall, the Third North Wall, to enclose this expansion. Opinions have been divided on the course of this wall also, the rival claimants being a course on the line of the present north wall and one further north which includes the line of defensive masonry just south of the St. George's compound and excavated by Sukenik and Mayer. Until recently opinions were fairly evenly divided, but recent excavations by Dr. J. B. Hennessy seem to show that the line was approximately that of the present north wall, and remains can be clearly seen near the Damascus Gate. It still remains, however, to decide what exactly the "Sukenik-Mayer line" was. Even if we assume that the city of Agrippa extended only as far north as the present north wall, this is still

5 K. M. Kenyon, *P.E.Q.* (1964, 1965, 1966).

a large increase in area. Josephus does say, though, that not all of the Bezetha Quarter was actually built up, but spaces were left for future expansion, showing considerable forethought in the planning department of the Jewish king. This first-century expansion does rather suggest that even at the time of Christ, which was only shortly before the reign of Agrippa, the built-up area had extended beyond the Second North Wall and might cast some doubts on whether the Holy Sepulcher area was still in use as a cemetery.

The population of Jerusalem at the time of the war with Rome must have been considerably larger than that under Nehemiah. We have an estimate from Josephus of 2,700,000 "clean" persons in the city at Passover time (Wars, VI, 9), but this must have consisted — even if the figure is accurate, which is doubtful — largely of pilgrims rather than native inhabitants. Josephus also

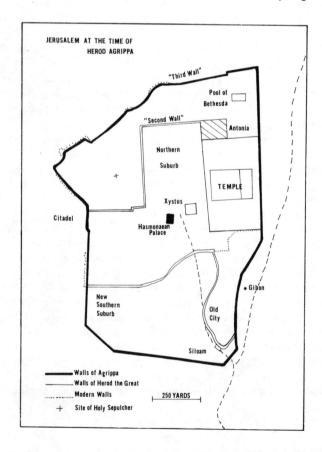

quotes Hecataeus who gives a figure of 120,000 for the normal population (Contra Apion, 1, 22). This figure is quite likely to be correct, considering the area which was built up. Modern scholars such as Heichelheim and Rops have estimated a population of about 100,000 but it is not easy to make an accurate statement because we are uncertain as to the area under public buildings and the actual density of private housing. It is clear, nonetheless, that from the return after the Exile, Jerusalem grew steadily in size and spread from the confines of the Ophel hill to the north and eventually, under Herod Agrippa, onto the southwestern hill also. Thus there is a movement of the city in the direction of the main trade routes and around the national cultural focus, the Temple. Unlike most European towns, the city did not develop around the original site, so that Ophel had by the first century A.D. ceased to be the civic core but had become a peripheral suburb.

BYZANTINE AND MEDIAEVAL JERUSALEM

The disastrous wars with Rome proved to be the turning point in the history of Jerusalem, because after lying waste for several years it was completely rebuilt in A.D. 132 as a new city with new walls, a new plan, a new site, and a new population. To the Romans, it was plain that the Jewish resistance in Jerusalem was so strong because of the religious nature of that city and its Temple, and so a successful attempt was made to eradicate all that was Jewish in Jerusalem and to turn it into a Gentile city. It became a colony with a legionary force camped in it, with the name of Aelia Capitolina.

Of the population of this colonial city we have no literary evidence, and little is said of Aelia until Byzantine times in the contemporary literature. Under the new colonists, it was probably reduced to the status of a small provincial administrative and market center, and there could have been little to attract a large population. The area it covered is, however, a little easier to assess, for it is practically certain that the new walls followed approximately the line of the present Old City walls, built by Suleiman. This would give a total area of about seventy acres, which can be reduced to sixty acres of residential settlement by excluding the Temple area (eight acres) which became a temple to Jupiter and the legionary headquarters (two acres). This would probably have held 18,000 people *at most,* but under the conditions of Roman town planning the number is more likely to have been 10,000.

For Byzantine times, we have good evidence from literary sources, excavations and for the first time, from contemporary maps. The Madaba Mosaic Map, although not easy to interpret, gives us an outline plan which enables us to learn something of the size of the city in the fourth century A.D. It appears that the walls followed approximately the line of the present ones, although there could have been an extension onto the southwest hill where a large building is shown, which could be the Byzantine Caiaphas's house, mentioned by the Bordeaux Pilgrim. Certainly by the next century, we read of a considerable spread of population onto the Mount of Olives and the southwest hill, now generally known as Mt. Zion to the pilgrims. There the enthusiastic church building program of Eudoxia, who also repaired the city walls and probably extended them to encircle the southwest hill, attracted large numbers. There are also remains of Byzantine buildings north of Jerusalem, giving a pic-

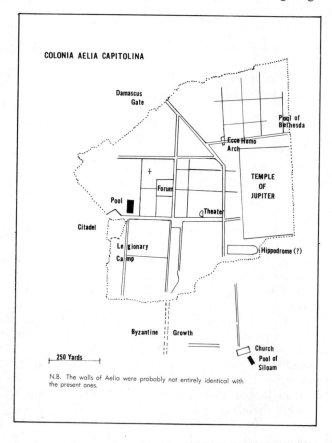

COLONIA AELIA CAPITOLINA

Damascus Gate

Pool of Bethesda

Ecce Homo Arch

+

Forum

TEMPLE OF JUPITER

Pool

Theater

Citadel

Legionary Camp

Hippodrome (?)

Byzantine Growth

250 Yards

Church

Pool of Siloam

N.B. The walls of Aelia were probably not entirely identical with the present ones.

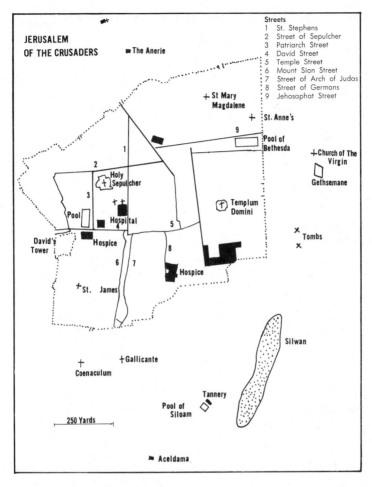

JERUSALEM
OF THE CRUSADERS ■ The Anerie

Streets
1 St. Stephens
2 Street of Sepulcher
3 Patriarch Street
4 David Street
5 Temple Street
6 Mount Sion Street
7 Street of Arch of Judas
8 Street of Germans
9 Jehosaphat Street

+ St Mary
Magdalene

+ St. Anne's

9

Pool of
Bethesda

+ Church of The
Virgin

Gethsemane

1

2

Holy
Sepulcher

3

+ +
Templum
Domini

Pool

+ +
Hospital

x
Tombs
x

4

5

David's
Tower

Hospice

8

6   7

Hospice

+ St. James

Silwan

+
Coenaculum

+ Gallicante

Tannery

Pool of
Siloam

250 Yards

➤ Aceldama

ture of a pronounced growth which took the city to its largest
extent prior to modern times. While it is clear that the areal
extent of the new Jerusalem was large, it is very difficult to estimate the population of the Byzantine city. The urban sprawl
covered an area probably larger than that in the time of Agrippa,
but much of the housing was outside the walls and the density
of residential building was probably not as great as that in Jewish times. In addition, a large acreage must have been occupied
by churches and other public buildings.

More information is available for Arab and Crusader Jerusalem, and although it is not always very exact, it is plain that
the city shrank in size. There are a few comparative statements,
such as one from Istakhri and Ibn Haukal that Jerusalem is
"nearly as large as Ramleh" but this is not really very helpful.

Mukaddasi, writing in the tenth century, writes at length about his native city and says "among provincial towns none is larger than Jerusalem and many capitals are in fact smaller." Later he goes on to say that Jerusalem is smaller than Mecca and larger than Medina. We do get a more precise figure for the Crusader period from Nasir-i-Khusrau, who gives the city a population of 20,000 men, although some have considered this too large a figure. Nasir also gives the information that up to 20,000 visitors were present during the first days of the pilgrimage, which indicates that the population increased considerably during religious festivals. For the twelfth century, useful figures are available from Beha ed-Din, which appear to corroborate Nasir's population figure. Beha gives statistics for the ransoming of the inhabitants of Jerusalem after its surrender to Saladin. The ransom set was ten Tyrian dinars per head for men; five for women and one for children. The total ransom collected was 220,000 dinars. Now if we assume that each family consisted of 1 man, 1 woman and 2 children (this latter figure might have been larger of course), then the average family paid seventeen dinars, which gives a total of 12,941 families, or 26,000 adults. Added to this were 3,000 Moslem prisoners in the city and 60,000 soldiers giving a total population at the time of siege of 90,000 or so.

It seems that throughout the early Middle Ages and the Crusader period, the city remained largely confined to the old walls, and had a civilian population of 20-30,000. It is interesting that there seems to have been no vast increase in either area or population under the Latin Kingdom. There are a large number of maps available which appear to show that the city was largely confined to the walls, although there were a large number of churches on the Mount of Olives. The Coenaculum is shown outside the walls on the map from The Hague (1170) and on the Paris map (c. 1160) and, neither does there appear to be an expansion of the walled area to the north, for the Stuttgart map shows both Mt. Zion and St. Stephen's Church firmly outside the walls.

There is, however, the problem of the line of wall shown on Marino Sanuto's map of the early fourteenth century. This map shows the older walls on the present line with an extension to the south covering Mount Zion. It has been suggested that some walls found by Bliss and Dickie are the remains of this wall and they are of Crusader date. Now it is quite logical that the city should expand to the south during the Crusader period, with the great increase due to pilgrimages, but this wall is not shown on the twelfth-century maps. If it is of Crusader date, then it is late. The insecurity which prevailed through most of the Crusader period would render any residential growth outside the city walls very vulnerable, and it seems that although there was a slight rise in the city's population it was largely confined within the walls. Benjamin of Tudela, called Jerusalem "a small city strongly fortified with three walls," having a "numerous population," but Mt. Zion, according to this Jewish traveler, was uninhabited except for a church, on his visit in 1163. Of course Sanuto could have drawn his wall to show the extent of the city in the time of Christ, for it was typical of mediaeval maps of the Holy Land that they obtained their data from the Bible and not from contemporary field observations. However, Siguli, who also wrote in the fourteenth century, describes Jerusalem as full of houses and people, and it appears that there was a neglect of the city's fortifications in the later Arab period, so the old walls probably had less of a restrictive influence on urban spread. In such conditions, a temporary wall around a small suburb on Mt. Zion is quite a possible feature, especially as at one time it held the Latin headquarters and therefore needed some security against any possible Moslem attacks.

OTTOMAN AND MODERN JERUSALEM

With the conquest of Jerusalem by the Ottoman Turks and the rebuilding of the old walls, we enter a new era. This era is marked by a profound decline in pilgrimages to Jerusalem and also in the size and population of the city, followed, after three centuries, by a boom in both, which is still in progress. It is an era also marked by a great increase in accurate travelers' reports and in detailed statistics.

For the sixteenth century city, the best source of information is the Turkish cadastral surveys. These give figures of 7,365 tax paying households and 1,254 exempt households, plus 516 bachelors, i.e. a figure of 9,135 for the Liwa of Jerusalem. This would give an adult population of about 20,000, which is not very large. The figures for Jerusalem city are 1,533 households plus 183 bachelors (there seems to have been no spinsters!), i.e. approximately 8,000 adults in the years 1533-9. By 1553-4, it had risen to 2,621 households plus 285 bachelors, i.e. over 13,500 adults. This is assuming that the present number of five adults per household was also the norm at that time but this still represents a large drop in population compared with previous centuries making the city smaller than Safed, Gaza, and others in the country. The area of Jerusalem remained confined by the walls, and even within the walls, many open spaces seem to have been visible. Few travelers found it impressive. Niebuhr regarded it as only a small town, and he had traveled widely enough to be able to make useful comparisons. His map, though not as detailed or accurate as his others of towns in the Middle East, shows little settlement outside the walls. Evidently, he was not impressed with the eighteenth century city.[6] Browne estimated its population as 18-20,000 at the end of the same century, but compared with later figures, this may seem a bit high. A more detailed breakdown of the population was given by Edward Robinson, the American scholar, for the city of the 1830's. He rejects the then-contemporary estimate of 15,000 for the number of resident "Franks" (as Europeans were called) and regards the figure as more like 11,000. As this was based on the recent taxation and conscription enumerations, it may be quite accurate. The total figures given by Robinson are:

Moslems	4,500
Jews	3,000
Christians	3,500
	11,000

To this he adds 500 for the monasteries. Another estimate of that period was that of Schulz, who gave a figure of 15,000. During the times of pilgrimage, of course, the total number within the walls increased, but the number of visitors even at Easter seems to have been low at the beginning of the last century. Ritter figured that only 10,000 pilgrims visited the city at Easter and adds that this figure is "small compared with that of former years."

It seems that the population was certainly not thick on the ground. There was so much land not built up that Robinson described the slope of the hill in the northeast part of the Old City as being in gardens and fields, while Warburton referred to Jerusalem as a collection of villages. Apart from the northeastern part of the city, the part of the present Jewish Quarter just west of the Haram enclosure was covered in rubbish and prickly pear.

The increase in population and area of the city in the second half of the nineteenth century is all the more remarkable after considering its low state throughout the preceding few centuries.

---

6 I. W. J. Hopkins, *Cartographic Journal* (December, 1967).

In 1858, the Mishkenot Sheananian settlement was built outside
the walls and a start was made in the expansion to the north
and west. In 1864, however, the population was still only about
15,000 although by 1870 Conder could figure it at 21,000. Even
so, this was not large when compared with the 175,000 of
Damascus and 70,000 of Beirut. Nablus and Hebron were not far
behind Jerusalem with 13,000 and 9,000 inhabitants respectively.
However, by the 1880's, the population seems to have been
getting nearer the 30,000 mark and the city, with more modern
housing densities, covered 200 acres. The Zionist immigrations
began to make a pronounced difference in the growth. By
1912, when Watson could estimate the population at 68,000, the
area covered by the city had extended far beyond the Old City
walls and a completely new city was being constructed to
the northwest. The maps which were published in the last
quarter of the nineteenth century show an increasing growth
of building both outside and inside the Old City, while the Russian Compound and the new Jewish buildings to the northwest
gave Jerusalem a broader and less confined appearance.

For the years since the British occupation of the city in 1917,
we have an urban growth well documented by maps and statistics. The area grew rapidly as the western expansion continued under the pressure of Jewish immigration, while Arab

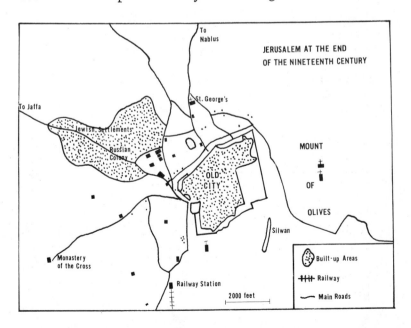

suburbs developed to the north and east. Under the security of
British rule, and with the growth of a new tourist trade, the
city's population grew rapidly from 50,000 in 1918 to 62,578
in 1922, 90,503 in 1931 (of which 51,222 were Jews). Of the
1931 total, over 25,000 were in the Old City, and the rest outside,
while the whole Jerusalem area, outside the municipal boundaries,
also showed large increases. These increases were only matched
by those in the Jaffa region. The attraction of Jerusalem for the
Jewish immigrants played a large part in this, of course, but
there was also an increase in the Arab population, for being
the seat of the Mandate government and the country's commercial center, there were a large number of jobs available.

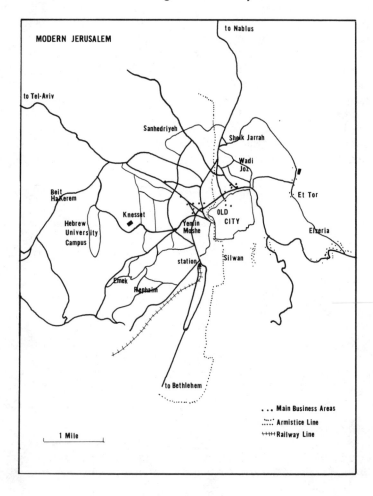

Following the division of Palestine in 1948, the twin cities of eastern and western Jerusalem continued on their separate ways. On the Jordanian side of the armistice line, there was an increased growth to the north of the Old City, especially in the Wadi Joz, and on and around the Mount of Olives. The built-up area now extends along the Jerusalem–Amman highway all the way to Bethany in the east. There was also an extension of the built-up area on the wasteland to the south of the Old City, which caused considerable concern to those engaged in archaeological "digs" in this area. The old Ophel and lower Tyropoeon valley areas are now completely built over by private houses. Inside the Old City, there still are many open spaces, including some patches of waste ground inside Herod's Gate in the northeast, and in the Jewish Quarter. These, together with the large number of churches in the Old City, do not make it overcrowded and most tourists comment on its pleasant atmosphere. The Israeli city developed rapidly to the west as far as Ein Karem and now covers a very large area, because in general it has been planning policy to build only on the ridges and leave the valleys as open space. This provides a pleasant atmosphere in the western suburbs, but means that the urban area now extends three miles to the west, for a population of more than 300,000. The Arab part of Jerusalem has a population of nearly 70,000.

It can thus be seen that the area covered by Jerusalem and its population size has varied enormously in the past, being governed largely by the security situation and in part by the amount of pilgrim activity. When the later trade has been active, as in the Herodian period, the Byzantine period, the Crusader period, the later Middle Ages and the modern period, then the city's population has increased and filled up the gaps within the city walls and spilled over into the hills and valleys around. At times of economic depression or political insecurity, the size of the city has dwindled, grass appeared within the city walls and its people declined in numerical strength to the size of an ordinary provincial town. At the present time, Jerusalem is developing as never before and its areal extent today is such as could not have been dreamed of before, even by Herod Agrippa.

The People

Finally, a brief look at the present population might help us to appreciate the heterogeneous nature of this city's people.

Jerusalem has come once more under one government and the eastern and western suburbs have been forcibly — and not too happily — united together and with the Old City. The population is very mixed and always has been since the present city was "founded" by Hadrian.

The Jews have been in Jerusalem since the city was taken by David, although they were excluded from the city during the Exile in Babylon and after the foundation of Aelia Capitolina until the city became Christian. It appears at one time that they may have lived in the northeast quarter of the Old City, which used to be called the "Juiverie," but the traditional Jewish Quarter lies to the southwest of the Haram enclosure. The Jews who lived in the city during the Ottoman period were generally of the Orthodox school of thought, and many writers testify to their fanatic zeal for their faith. Both Ashkenazim and Sephardim were represented; there were Karaites also. Today, the Jews live entirely in the western part of the city and present a very mixed racial society. Apart from the large numbers of European Jews who would fit in perfectly in any city in Europe or America, there are Yemenite Jews and Falasha Jews from Ethiopia, Russian Jews and Indian Jews. Until the Mandate period, the Jews were always in a minority in the city, but now they represent by far the largest group although they cannot claim Jerusalem quite as exclusively as their own as they could in the time of the kings.

The Arab population of Jerusalem could quite possibly claim to be its first inhabitants, for the Jebusites no doubt have their descendants in the Palestinian peasantry. The Arabs are also mixed in racial features and include descendants not only of the ancient Canaanites, but also of the Crusaders, and some are of true Arab stock. They are divided into Moslem and Christian groups. The Moslems entered the city in the seventh century with its capture by Omar, and they have generally been the dominant group in the city since then until the Jewish immigrations. There have at times been a few non-Arab Moslems in Jerusalem, including Indians and Negroes, but today practically all of the permanent Moslem inhabitants are Arabs. Many of them live in the Old City, where they tend to congregate to the west and north of the Haram, although the traditional "quarters" do not represent a hard and fast division of religions. Most of the inhabitants of the suburbs to the south, including Silwan, are Moslem. In general they have not been so prominent as the Christians and Jews in civic life, often suffering from a poor education and fatalistic notions of life. A far lower percentage

ARAB JERUSALEM. The main shopping center on Saladin Street is viewed from Herod's Gate.

of Moslems are shopkeepers and financiers than is the case with the Christians. Nevertheless, as they are the predominant group in the Arab city, the place is very quiet on a Friday morning, which is the Moslem day of prayer. In general, the Moslems have been tolerant of their Christian and Jewish neighbors, although from time to time government intolerance has made life miserable for the minority groups.

The Christian Arabs have generally been strong in influence if not in numbers and at times have had a major say in the affairs of the city. A large part of this influence has come from their better education, and Christian Arabs have generally been able to take influential government posts and accumulate wealth through trade and commerce. A large number of the shops today are owned by Armenian and Arab Greek Christians. Of course, they have often had the backing of the foreign religious communities who, particularly in the last decades of Turkish rule, claimed the protection of European powers and enjoyed under the millet system, a fair degree of autonomy.

Of the Arab Christians, the largest group is the Greek Orthodox Church, which is led by a largely Greek clergy. It is the only church with real roots in the villages of Palestine and thus is not just a pilgrim community, but an active native denomination. Of the other Eastern churches in the city, the Armenians have been in Jerusalem for many centuries and have been large enough to have their own quarter, but they have no following in the countryside. There is also a small Syrian Orthodox community in the city and Coptic groups who are largely there to look after pilgrims. Similarly, the Roman Catholic presence in Jerusalem, although often dominant because of the power of her protective countries, France and Italy, and her "Western" outlook, is largely involved in looking after the holy sites and taking care of pilgrims. There are some Roman Catholic schools, but few native followers. The Protestants are small in number, but there are a number of native churches and missions in the city, in particular, the Anglican, Baptist, and Pentecostal churches having the largest increase in numbers of all the Christian groups.

For many centuries the ethnic and religious groups in Jerusalem have tried to be self containing and have collected in geographical groupings in the "Quarters" and there has been little proselytizing. The result is a mosaic of race and creed from all parts of the Middle East and Europe, which has made the population of Jerusalem probably the most interesting of any city in the world.

VII

WITHIN THE CITY (1)

(The Biblical Period)

Mention has already been made of some of the internal divisions of Jerusalem, but in the final chapters we shall consider in detail the morphology of the city — its streets, suburbs, public buildings, and the location of the various facets of its commercial and social life. With the advent in modern times of the science of town planning, it is easier for us to understand the importance of studying the make-up of an urban community in terms of locational factors and the historical processes behind the urban land use pattern. In the case of Jerusalem, the importance of the past in influencing the present can be seen only too well. Yet the break which came about with the Jewish wars of the first and second centuries A.D. so altered the morphology of Jerusalem that continuity between the Biblical period and modern times is largely broken. A few locations remained the same — the Temple area on Mt. Moriah is the main one — but generally speaking, the city of today has quite different historical foundations from that of Herod Agrippa. Consequently in this chapter we shall, after making a few general observations, concentrate on the city of ancient times and discuss the molding of the city as it was just before the Roman legions marched to destroy it. In the next chapter, the making of the modern Old City and its immediate suburbs will be discussed.

Jerusalem, as we have seen, has occupied throughout its history the promontory of Turonian limestone bounded by the valleys of the Kidron and Hinnom, only recently spilling over into neighboring hills and valleys. The city has not, however, always occupied the same part of that promontory. In fact it is

115

rather interesting that the Old City of today is almost a fringe suburb of the New City which stretches out to the west; and the Ophel and Zion hills to the south, once occupied by the streets and houses of the city of Herod, are largely rural. In this change, one can distinguish three main trends:

1) A movement of the city as a whole in a southeast to northwest direction. The original Jebusite and Davidic city was on Ophel with later extensions to the north and west. There was little extension to the south, and we are now fairly sure that there was no extension onto the southwest hill until the first century A.D. Aelia Capitolina was established to the north of the original site, further up the Turonian promontory, with expansions in Byzantine times to the north, east and south. Towards the end of the Ottoman era, the city again developed away from its core, in a north/northwest direction, but not to the south or east. In recent years, while there has been some building on the southern and eastern flanks, the greatest development has again been further northwards along the Turonian promontory and further to the west. Thus instead of remaining as the central areas, the original city of David and the Old City of the Middle Ages, have found themselves in "eccentric" locations on the fringe of the total urban area.

2) Accompanying this trend (or perhaps spearheading it), has been a movement of the urban "core." This "core" area consists of the markets, main shops, finance houses and all those commercial and administrative functional units which make up the "Central Business District" (C.B.D.) of the modern western city.[1] While the concept of the C.B.D. has been in general only worked out in the context of European and American cities, it is equally applicable to Oriental cities, for the locational factors operating remain the same in each. The town center of Jerusalem was originally on Ophel and probably in the center of the city or near a gate. Gate locations for markets were common because of time-saving factors and the funneling of traffic through these few entry points into the city. These gate locations tended to pull the city towards the periphery by encouraging settlement in and outside the main gates. The main gates of Jerusalem leading to the populous districts and the districts from which the merchants came were in the north and so the core area of the city seems to have migrated north in Biblical times and into the "Mishneh" Quarter on the site of the present

---

1 See J. Beaujeu-Garnier and G. Chabot, *Urban Geography*, p. 299 ff.

Muristan. In Aelia, this area was central and so encouraged the C.B.D. to remain there, but the pull of the gates became operative again when the pilgrim trade got under way and traders moved to the main routeways into the city. The modern business districts of Jerusalem had crystallized with the presence of the armistice line into the Jaffa Road — Shlomzion Hamalka area in the Jewish city and the Nablus Road — Jericho Road area in the Arab city, although the Suq Khan es-Zeit still has important functions. Thus the urban commercial "core" has moved from Ophel to locations which are far to the north and west.

3) A third factor evident, is the stability of one important feature in Jerusalem — the Temple area. This has remained constant as a religious site and has exerted a "pull" on city growth to attract it at first northwards and then to help hold it back within the walls of the Old City. Its economic and social attractions must have been one of the main motives in attracting settlement to the west of its walls when the bulk of the city was to the south, for it would have been of great advantage to be living near the center of religious, financial, and cultural life in the city. Certainly traders must have taken early advantage of a location near its gates, as the main entrance streets today are lined with retailers. Its attraction for the Moslem and Jewish inhabitants of the city gave a location within the walls the advantage over one outside and thus held back any tendency for urban growth to the west and north until population pressure brought the sudden expansion of built-up area into existence.

The movement to the northwest can thus be seen to be under several influences. Physical factors have played their part as well as the economic and social ones, as was observed in Chapter 2. The nineteenth-century geographer, Ritter, concluded that: "The city was always confined: it could not extend itself down into the ravines, it could in no way reach beyond them: the only opportunity which it had of enlarging itself was towards the north." The superiority of the Turonian as a building stone and a soil formerly confined development to the promontory. The water supply problem has also influenced growth, for while the only sources were the Virgin's Fountain and Job's Well, no-one could afford to live far away from the Ophel ridge. But with the improved technology of Roman times, with better cisterns and a piped supply, families could move to more spacious quarters and hence we get the first real movement north and west in the Herodian era. The better water supply west of the city must have been one factor influencing settlement on that side at the end of the last century and has discouraged building east of the Mount of Olives. However, the main influences on this northwest spread are social and economic. It is very noticeable that the growth of a city tends to be towards those neighbors with which it has the closest ties. Jerusalem's ties with Jaffa to the west and Samaria and Caesarea via the route to the north, have been far stronger than those requiring use of the southern and eastern exits from the city. The pronounced tendency for the city to develop to the north and west is in large measure an expression of these links.

BIBLICAL JERUSALEM

Zones of Movement

The skeleton of a city is formed around its zones of movement — the streets and footpaths which carry the population and the city's visitors from one place to another. They are closely linked with the position of the markets and public buildings, and tend to run towards these from the residential suburbs. However, as we shall see in the next chapter, streets can also determine the location of commercial features and so the relationship between zones of movement and areas of commerce and residence is a two-way one. In order to build up a better picture of the internal workings of Jerusalem, it is probably best to begin with the zones of movement and then move on to the static areas completing the urban body.

The streets of ancient Jerusalem have been long buried by the rubble above or washed away by the erosive action of storm waters. Unlike structures of stone which can last many centuries, streets in old Oriental cities were rarely built deeply or solidly enough to survive the subsequent "quarrying" which always went on when one city was built on the ruins of an older settlement. Little remains of the streets of Biblical Jerusalem apart from some stepped streets on the eastern slopes of Mt. Zion, which probably date from the first century A.D. There are also two remains of possible viaducts across the Tyropoeon, from the Temple to the suburbs west of the valley, known as Wilson's Arch and Robinson's Arch. The rest must be mainly intelligent guesswork from what we know of the location of the gates of the ancient city and the main public places. It is quite likely that there was a street running down the Tyropoeon valley (probably on the slope rather than the valley bottom) to take major traffic from the Pool of Siloam area and the Ophel ridge

to the suburbs west of the Temple. Originally, this was probably
the route from the City of David to the north and west and
thus the major entry/exit artery of the city. Across this, the two
viaducts provided some east-west movement into and away from
the Temple, the upper one (Wilson's Arch) being in existence
in Hasmonaean times and the lower (Robinson's Arch) in Herodian times. Of the streets of the original small city on Ophel
we have little indication. The Old Testament, however, does
give us some details about the gates of the city, especially that
precise-minded governor, Nehemiah. Again, it is to him that we
turn for the details. His famous description of the topography
of the city seen on his night ride is worth quoting in full:

> And I went out by night by the valley gate, even toward
> the dragon's well, and to the dung gate, and viewed the
> walls of Jerusalem, which were broken down, and the
> gates thereof were consumed with fire. Then I went on
> to the fountain gate and to the king's pool: but there was
> no place for the beast that was under me to pass. Then
> went I up in the night by the brook, and viewed the wall;
> and I turned back, and entered by the valley gate, and
> so returned. — Neh. 2:13-15

The list of gates is enlarged upon in the following chapter
which tells of the actual rebuilding of the walls, and enables us
to locate some of the gates with a reasonable certainty. The
gates which are easiest to tie down are those named after some
topographical feature: the Valley Gate; the Fountain Gate;
the Water Gate. The Valley Gate presumably led into one of the
valleys. Those scholars who held that the city of Nehemiah em-
braced both sides of the Tyropoeon valley have sometimes taken
the Valley Gate to open onto the Hinnom, but if we now assume — as seems most likely — that the city was still largely confined to the Ophel hill, the gate must have opened into the
Kidron or the Tyropoeon. Another mention of this gate is in II
Chron. 26:9, which mentions the building of towers here, so it
was presumably a strong point. The Water Gate and the Fountain Gate must be located, one at the Pool of Siloam, and
the other near Gihon. The East Gate must plainly be in the
eastern wall and the Fish Gate is likely to be in the north,
from where the fish merchants came. If we follow the account
in Nehemiah 3, bearing the above in mind, we see a circular pattern. The Sheep Gate is likely to be in the north because there
are good arguments for the location of a gate of that name in
Herodian times in that quarter. As Nehemiah records that it

was built by the priests, it was most likely a Temple gate and so would be found in the northern wall of the Temple enclosure. The next gate mentioned is the Fish Gate, which was probably situated just south of the Temple enclosure and was probably the main gate leading out to the cities of the coast and Samaria. In the western line of wall there were then three more gates before reaching the Fountain Gate. This was almost certainly located just above the Pool of Siloam, for directly after it are mentioned the "Pool of Shelah" and also the King's Garden and the "stairs that go down from the city of David" which have been found at "Pointe Sud," the name sometimes given by archaeologists to the southern tip of the Ophel ridge. Consequently, the Old Gate, the Valley Gate and the Dung Gate were probably found at intervals in the western wall between the Fish Gate and the Fountain Gate. After rounding the tip of Ophel, the next gate was the Water Gate, almost certainly near Gihon. The Horse Gate, which is mentioned next, would appear to be a gate in the wall north of Gihon, probably leading to the king's palace (hence the name, from troop movements, etc.), although on the basis of the mention of a "horses' entry" in II Kings 11:16, some have suggested that it was a gate connecting the Temple to the palace. The East Gate and the Hammiphkad Gate are most likely Temple gates. The above circuit is not the only possible interpretation of Nehemiah 3, but perhaps the best "fit" of topography and text. Within the walls, the street pattern was most likely haphazard, and probably consisted of alleyways linking up the houses with the public markets and buildings.

By the time of Herod Agrippa, the city had expanded considerably, and new gates were built. New gates in the north, such as the "Mishneh Gate," and the Ephraim Gate were built and the Valley Gate was probably "moved" onto Mt. Zion. One gate which has caused much discussion is the Gennath Gate, because as mentioned previously, it is a vital link in the description by Josephus of the course of the Second North Wall and hence effects the authenticity of the Holy Sepulcher. We know from Josephus that this gate was in the First Wall and the Second Wall began near it. The name *Gennath* means garden and hence it probably led into gardens which probably surrounded the city (see Chapter 8, p. 143). Scholars holding the long or the stepped courses for the Second North Wall have generally placed this gate near the Citadel tower at the present Jaffa Gate. This is logical, as it would then lead out into the Hinnom valley where the gardens would most likely be located. The excavations in the Muristan under Dr. Kenyon might at first sight suggest that this gate be located further east,[2] but as we shall see later, the evidence is not complete. Anyway, there was an entry into the city at the northwest corner and the streets would have led in from all the gates towards the commercial quarter just west of the Temple. The direction of the streets on the map is largely conjectural. Professor Avi-Yonah's now famous model of the city in the first century A.D. shows a grid-iron pattern on Mt. Zion, one of the new suburbs, which is quite likely. The pattern in the "lower class" quarters in the Tyropoeon and around Ophel are likely, however, to be more haphazard and irregular. The main artery is likely to have been the Tyropoeon as already suggested, linking a gate near the Pool of Siloam to the northern gates and leading through the main commercial and industrial quarter, with certain cross-roads running east-west, linking the through route with the suburbs.

Areas of Commerce and Industry

Within the skeletal framework of the gates and streets can be fitted the location of the areas of activity and residence. Where did the commuter of Agrippa's city go to work each morning, and where did his wife go to shop? Again, we lack much precise information because the Bible, our main source, is not a textbook on urban geography and the Old Testament prophets were not concerned with leaving to posterity a detailed breakdown of the Central Business District of the Holy City.

Of considerable importance in the urban geography of ancient towns were the open squares which could be used as markets, or places for addressing crowds, or as places simply to go and gossip. We know nothing of the squares of the early city, but there is a clue in Nehemiah 8:16 of two possible public squares. Mention is there made of "the broad place of the water gate and the broad place of the gate of Ephraim." As we have seen, the Water Gate is likely to have been located near Gihon, as this would be a daily meeting point for the women of the town. Such a square is probable, although it was almost certainly outside the gate if it was close to the spring itself. The Ephraim Gate, by its name, must have been to the north of the city, probably a postern or small entrance in the

---

2 Kenyon, P.E.Q. (1965).

western wall of the Temple. This square is located by Simons on the hill where the Holy Sepulcher stands. The excavations in the Muristan by the British School of Archaeology have shown that at least part of this area was leveled off in the seventh century B.C. and remained unbuilt upon until the creation of Aelia. This would suggest that this may well have been part of the "broad place of the Gate of Ephraim," although it could also have been on the floor of the Tyropoeon. Extra-mural sites were popular for open spaces, as they did not take up valuable space inside the walls, and merchants did not have to pay dues. Unfortunately, the report on the British School's excavation does not tell us the size of their "dig" in this spot, so we cannot tell whether this find is significant or not. From Luke 23, where a crowd was able to gather in front of the Antonia fortress to be addressed by Pilate, it appears that there must have been an open space there too, by Herodian times, probably as a central meeting point for the Bezetha Quarter.

One specific public place we know of in Hellenistic and Roman Jerusalem was the Xystus, mentioned by Josephus as being between the Citadel and the Temple and by the First Wall. It was possibly in the Tyropoeon and was used as an open space for public gathering, and it may also have been used as a market. Avi-Yonah places the town hall next to the Xystus and, with a very central location, it could well have been the central meeting point of the whole city with the same general functions which modern town squares and city centers have. The main road down the Tyropoeon would be just to the east and the Xystus would be within easy access of all the city suburbs.

These open squares were frequently used for the markets, but not all markets were of the temporary type, as many were permanent shops in streets, usually grouped according to the nature of the retailing. These streets are known in the Arab world as the suqs or bazaars and the specialization of these retailing centers can still be seen today. The tailors would have their shops in one street and the bakers and goldworkers and leatherworkers, etc. would all have their special street or area where they worked and sold. As in the case of ethnic groupings, security was probably the chief motive for this locational phenomenon, especially as in ancient times a large number of traders were foreigners. The market of the early town was thus not quite as centralized as the modern C.B.D., and hence the determination of an urban "core" area is difficult. Nevertheless, there are certain factors which can be seen at work which help to produce a pattern in market location. The usual sites for markets in ancient cities were:

1) *By the royal palace.* As George Adam Smith pointed out, the kings of ancient cities usually invited merchants to settle in the town under their patronage. A location by the actual palace was of considerable benefit to the merchant as it ensured that a good constant trade was near at hand either from the inmates of the palace or the constant stream of visitors to the royal court, while there was probably a greater security under the palace walls than elsewhere in the city. Thus we find in Jerusalem's history a large number of markets located near "David's Tower," and no doubt in ancient times there were also markets near the royal palace south of the Temple.

2) *The Temple* also attracted trade. As we have seen, the Temples were generally the first banks and the Deuteronomic requirement for pilgrims to buy all their needs in Jerusalem (including the sacrifices), caused many of the priests to engage in trade near or even in the Temple. The most striking example of this is in the New Testament when Jesus entered the Temple and "cast out all them that sold and bought in the Temple, and overthrew the tables of the money-changers, and the seats of them that sold the doves" (Matt. 21:12). Other holy sites have had a similar attracting influence.

3) *Gates* have attracted traders also, because of lower rents on the periphery of the city, and the presence of more room. An extra-mural location is particularly attractive as in the old days dues were levied on trading within the city walls. Thus it might be that Nehemiah's complaint against the traders outside the walls was not just on moral grounds but because the civic government was thereby losing dues (Neh. 13:20-21). The most attractive gates for merchants were the northern and western gates because, in the case of Jerusalem, this was the direction from which most of them came (they were generally foreigners). These exits were also the busiest ones out of the city and were the gates most in use by pilgrims.

Taking these four considerations into account, the most likely place for the situation of a market in ancient Jerusalem would be to the west of the Temple, which would combine the pull of the holy sites with the attraction of the royal palace just to the south on Ophel, and in later times the Antonia fortress north of the Temple. After the Exile, the peripheral pull of the gates would take the market north to this same point and the city would follow.

Street trading seems to have been common in Biblical times, and this is possibly hinted at in Jeremiah 5:1 where the streets are linked with the "broad places" or squares. Jeremiah later mentions a baker's street (Jer. 37:21) and a potter's house (Jer. 18:2). Where they were is uncertain, although the latter was possibly in the lowest part of the Tyropoeon as the operative verb used here is "go down" and the Gate of the potsherds was probably in the lower Hinnom area. This location would be good because of the constant demand from women who had broken pitchers on the way to or from the Pool of Siloam or Job's Well. Zephaniah (1:11) mentions a Maktesh or market quarter of foreign merchants. The context would imply a location somewhere in the northern or northwestern part of the city:

> And in that day, saith the Lord, there shall be the noise of a cry from the fish gate, and a howling from the second quarter, and a great crashing from the hills. Howl, ye inhabitants of Maktesh, for all the people of Canaan are undone: all they that were laden with silver are cut off. — Zeph. 1:10-11

Josephus adds some information about this market. He says that the upper town was "styled by us the upper market place" (Wars, 5, 4.), and this would substantiate the suggested location of Zephaniah's Maktesh, a more exact location being probably the area of the present Muristan. The upper city was the Mt. Zion hill as opposed to the lower Ophel and Tyropoeon suburbs, but the southern part of this hill had by Josephus' time only recently become a residential suburb of "high class" and would be unlikely to have a market, so the best location is near the Muristan-upper Tyropoeon area. This is confirmed by another reference in Josephus, that when Titus had broken through the Second Wall, he entered "at that part of the new town where were the wool marts, the braziers shops and the clothes market . . ." (Wars 5, 8.). If we follow the short course for the Second Wall, this would place the market just east of the present Suq Khan es-Zeit and in the area immediately west of the Temple inside the northern gates, i.e. the location most to be expected. There is also a hint of a timber market in the area near the present Holy Sepulcher (Wars, 2.19) and, as Hanauer suggested, it certainly seems that there was a market on both sides of the wall in Herodian times. By the time of Agrippa, the locational pattern of retailing activity consisted of a large central market (and probably manufacturing) area stretching from the Temple across the Tyropoeon and onto the northern part of the Western ridge, with certain peripheral locations of street traders or stallholders — the fishmongers probably just outside the Fish Gate and the potters near the gate at the mouth of the Tyropoeon, and other traders at the other gates. The Temple itself would also have a large market geared to the pilgrim industry.

We have little information about the location of manufacturing industry in the ancient city, although it was probably centered in the same area as the market because many traders would have been retailers as well as manufacturers. In any case there would be considerable advantages in a manufacturer locating near his buyers. The textile industry probably flourished by supplying the wool and clothes markets mentioned by Josephus. There was a Fullers' Field outside the city (II Kings 18:17; Isa. 36:2) and ancient fullers' vats exist near Job's Well. The location of the Fullers' Field seems to have been near the walls and near the "conduit of the upper pool." With its need for a large supply of water, this trade was almost certainly confined to the main water supply points. Pottery manufacture is also an old industry, for a Gate of the Potters is mentioned in Jeremiah 11:2 and a Potter's Field in Matthew 27:7. The location of this industry, probably closely linked with the retailing side, was almost certainly in the lower Tyropoeon-Hinnom area.

Financial activities as we have seen, were probably largely centered around the Temple in ancient times, because apart from the monarchy, the Temple was the only institution with the cash resources to engage in banking, and the priests were the only literate section of the population until at least classical times. Money changers and other smaller financiers consequently located their activities in and around the Temple precincts.

It is unfortunate that we really have so little information about the actual location of commercial and manufacturing activity in Jerusalem, so that apart from recognizing that the main centers of such enterprises were the Maktesh quarter inside the Second Wall and the courts of the Temple, little more can be said.

Areas of Administrative Activity

Turning from commercial considerations, among the most important features of the geography of Jerusalem are the government buildings and the military headquarters. In Biblical times, government activity was generally concentrated in the king's palace. Here he ruled and here justice was meted out and the everyday affairs of state decided on. Solomon appears to have been the first to launch out on a multiplicity of government buildings. He constructed the "house of the king" south of the Temple, which is often taken to have been on the site of the present Al Aqsa mosque. He also built the House of the Forest of Lebanon (I Kings 7), which according to Josephus was built to "receive a multitude for judgments and for the decision of public business and to provide room for an assembly of men convened for cases of justice" (Ant., 5.2). It also seems that gold treasure was deposited there, so this building appears to have been a treasury in part and also an assize court and place of assembly. There was also a Porch of Judgment, but its location is uncertain, except that it was probably near the king's house on Ophel. It is likely, in fact, that the public buildings used for administration in pre-Exilic times were concentrated on the higher and wider part of Ophel just below the Temple, and thus they would dominate the city.

Herod the Great, that other prolific builder in Jerusalem, constructed for himself a palace south of the Citadel which was closely connected with it. This move marked a pronounced shift of administration from the eastern hill to the western hill, in line with the movement of both markets and the residential suburbs.

Closely linked with administration is the military activity, and often both of these functions have been in the same hands. Apart from the walls which defended the town, Jerusalem, in common with other ancient cities, had its fortresses or strong points where the ruler could defend himself not only against any foreign invaders, but against any rebellious elements in the city's population. We do not know the location of the early royal fortress in Jerusalem, although many writers have suggested that the name Zion refers to such a place. It probably refers to the whole complex of buildings south of the Temple, and it is likely that here there was also a fortress, probably part of the palace compound. It would separate the city from the Temple and guard both from outside attack. An early fortress over which there has been considerable debate is the Akra, which was built in Hellenistic times as a fortress to guard the city. It gave the Hasmonaeans considerable trouble before they captured it and completely razed it. Scholars have located it all over Jerusalem, but the favorite location is just south of the Haram wall. Here, near the site of Zion, it would be in a key position to control the Temple hill. In view of the fact that it "became a great trap, an ambush against the Sanctuary" (I Macc. 1:33-35), some scholars have located it on a higher elevation. Conder and many others placed the Akra on the hill on which the Holy Sepulcher now stands, but most writers now agree with George Adam Smith that the most likely place is somewhere on the eastern hill.

However, in the Herodian period, the military headquarters moved, with the palace, to the western hill. The new fortress of Herod, the Citadel, where that king built three towers called Hippicus, Phasael, and Mariamne, proved so effective that Hadrian took it over as the headquarters of the legionary forces in the city, and it has been retained as the main defensive point in Jerusalem ever since. It still presents the most complete structure left standing, dating from Biblical times. The other strong point in the Jerusalem of the first century A.D. was the Antonia fortress at the northwest corner of the Temple, which Herod built in order to watch the activities in the Temple below. It too has lasted to some extent over the centuries, and remains are now shown to visitors. Finally, Herod's deep suspicion of the local populace, caused him to devise an "in depth" defense policy. He then built the fortress of Herodium, still conspicuous on the skyline to the south of Jerusalem, as a retreat in case of difficulty.

Agricultural Areas

It has already been seen that despite the apparent strict division of town and country which the city walls represent, peasant and citizen were probably far more mixed in work and play than in modern society. The presence of gardens within the city walls was quite common, and in classical times Jerusalem must have appeared quite green, especially in the north. There, as Josephus informs us, there were many open spaces between the houses, as the Bezetha quarter was enclosed before it had become thickly settled. Before the advent of the tin can and the refrigerator, cities were much more dependent on fresh food supplies, and so even fields are frequently found mentioned in early descriptions of ancient and mediaeval cities. The advantages a farmer had with a location near a town, and the form this location is likely to have taken were first explained fully by a farmer-economist, Heinrich Von Thünen, who showed how crops which had a high cost of transport to market relative to price (e.g. heavy vegetables or perishable fruit) would be located nearer to a city than those which had a lower cost of transport or could be stored — wheat, wool, etc.[3] A farmer growing vegetables within or just outside the city walls obviously spends less time and therefore less money in getting his goods to market and can therefore undercut a competitor who lives in a village a couple of miles away. However, this does not mean that there is a continuous ring of market gardens outside the city walls, for questions of soil, slope and other considerations also influence the precise location. In Jerusalem, one would therefore expect the Kidron and Hinnom valleys, relatively well watered, with a depth of soil lacking on the hills, and close to the city, to be the main gardens of Jerusalem. Two locations seem to have been favored for gardens in the Kidron valley. One was in the stretch around Ophel, below the Virgin's Fountain and the other was below the Pool of Siloam. Both benefited from overflow from their respective water sources as well as normal runoff down the valley after winter rains. In the area below Siloam was probably located the King's Gardens. This garden is twice mentioned in connection with hasty exits from the city to flee to the desert, and a location here would suit that context best (II Kings 25:4; Jer. 39:4). Gethsemane is probably the most famous of Jerusalem's gardens, and the traditional spot below the Temple wall is probably correct. There are fewer indications as to the gardens in the Hinnom, except for the mention of the Gennath or Garden Gate by Josephus. This is most likely to be a gate leading down to vegetable gardens in the Hinnom below the Citadel, probably intended to supply that fortress with food. Of course if the gate be located further east, it provides evidence for the existence of gardens in the new enclosed northern suburb, just outside the market quarter. This would be a good location for a vegetable market, but it is not certain whether there would be sufficient water or depth of soil here to support one. If the Holy Sepulcher is authentically located it would show the existence of a garden/cemetery here, for John records that: ". . . in the place where he was crucified there was a garden; and in the garden a new tomb wherein was never man yet laid" (John 19:41). However, it seems unlikely that a cemetery should be built just outside the market, with a new suburb developing around it and that if it was there, that it should still be in use by men of the status of Joseph of Arimathea. If this area was used for gardens, then they would most likely be of the commercial type, for only then

---

3 H. von Thünen, *The Isolated State.*

would the cost of providing water (and perhaps also soil) justify itself. Gardens have been generally easier to maintain in the valleys, and hence most of the burial grounds seem to have been on the valley sides. However, no doubt some of the new inhabitants of the northern quarter considered it worth while to lay out gardens for their residences, but the specific naming of a city gate as the "Garden Gate" would suggest that it led to a vegetable garden or cemetery of some prominence, and this is only likely in the Hinnom valley.

Other gardens probably existed on the Mount of Olives to judge by the name of that hill and that of one of its villages, "Bethphage." Jesus cursed a fig tree on the way from Bethany to Jerusalem, but for reasons already given for Bezetha, the growth of vegetation is unlikely to have been thick, for even today away from the Kidron, the hill slopes have only scrub and trees. Within the city there were probably gardens, with the Bezetha quarter and the new quarter on the southwest hill prominent, but again water supply must have made extensive cultivation difficult. The king's residence in the Citadel had gardens attached, with an aqueduct to feed them, and it is likely that the Temple area was not without a touch of green (Ps. 52:8). In all, the city was probably much more pleasant in appearance than most modern conurbations, at least in the better class quarters.

Areas of Residence

This leads us to consider where the main residential areas were in fact located. Because most private houses were not constructed with the huge stone blocks which typify "Herodian" masonry, we have few remains and the location of such areas largely depends on negative evidence. Josephus divides the city into an Upper City and a Lower City (Wars, 5.4), with the Bezetha Quarter added to the north (Wars, 2.15). In the original city on Ophel the residential quarters were almost certainly on the southern part of the ridge, below the royal palaces and near the supplies of water. They were probably cramped and congested. By Agrippa's time the vast expansion of Jerusalem to the north and west had opened the city up and most of the new area was now taken up with residential quarters. The old quarters on Ophel and in the lower Tyropoeon valley were probably inhabited by the poorer classes, with the better class development on the top of the southwestern hill, later to be called Mt. Zion, and the northern quarter. Thus the residential areas spread around the Temple and commercial "core" area, but on the Turonian ridge where they could be defended by new walls obligingly built by Herod Agrippa. There seems to have been little expansion eastwards into the Kidron or onto the Mount of Olives, although from the Gospel accounts it seems that Bethany was regarded as within commuter distance of the city. The newer suburbs within the city were probably laid out on classical lines with gardens, or at least open spaces between villas and blocks of well-built houses. Somewhere in the city were the amusement sites, the amphitheatre and hippodrome in the first century A.D., most likely in or around the lower Tyropoeon within reach of the most densely settled suburbs.

THE TEMPLE

With the exception of the synagogues, of which there are few remains, the location of religious buildings in the city is limited in Biblical times to one — the Temple. This building and its courts dominated the entire city and in a sense also symbolized it. Among modern scholars there is no serious objector to the view that the Temple of Solomon stood over the Sakhra rock in approximately the same place as the present Dome of the Rock. However, in the nineteenth century there was much debate on the true site of the old Temple, with strong objections to the traditional site by the architect James Fergusson, who considered that the Dome of the Rock stood over the real site of the Holy Sepulcher. The original area of the Temple enclosure was much smaller than the Haram enclosure which we see today and presented a more nearly square appearance. It lasted until the destruction of Jerusalem by the Assyrians, but after the return from Exile, a second Temple was constructed. This reached its largest area in the reconstruction of Herod the Great who extended the total area and gave the place the form which it had when the city fell in A.D. 70. The altar and central shrines were surrounded by a series of courts, the inner one being confined to the priests. Then came the court of the Israelites for the men, and to the east of this was the court of the women. Beyond, was the court of the Gentiles, which in total amounted to half the area of the whole enclosure and surrounded the central courts on all sides. This was not so much because the Jews expected a large number of Gentile "tourists," but because most of the financial and other business was probably carried out in this outer court. From remains in the Haram walls, it seems that Herod's Temple was the same shape and area as the present Moslem sanctuary. From time to time other places had some sacred function, such as tombs of notaries[4] or the Topheth high place in the Hinnom valley and the synagogues, but the main religious activity was on the Moriah hill.

---

4 See for example, David's Tomb (Acts 2:29).

VIII

WITHIN THE CITY (2)

(The Growth of Modern Jerusalem)

The events of A.D. 70 when the Roman armies, after prolonged and bitter fighting, managed to take the last resisting quarter of Jewish Jerusalem, proved the dividing point of the city's history. The present Old City really dates back only as far as A.D. 132, when the Roman city of Aelia Capitolina was founded, for just the site of the Temple and the tower of the Citadel were left recognizable, continuing through the vicissitudes of the Middle Ages. They still stand for the admiration of twentieth-century man. From the second century onwards, however, information on the geography of Jerusalem becomes much more profuse, and for certain periods there are a large number of contemporary accounts of the city and maps also, to help in fitting a picture together of the geographical organs within the civic body.

Zones of Movement

The lack of knowledge of the streets and gates of ancient Jerusalem which caused so much difficulty in the last chapter, scarcely exists in dealing with the new city, for it is almost certain that the walls, gates and streets of the present Old City are the direct descendants of the same features in Aelia Capitolina. The straightness of the main streets in Jerusalem is so unusual for an Oriental city (cf. Acre or Baghdad) that unless they were laid out in Crusader times (we have no record of this) they can only be the skeleton of the Roman colony. This is confirmed by the Madaba Mosaic Map, which clearly shows the two north-south thoroughfares of the city, forking south of

132

THE DAMASCUS GATE, the main northern entry into the Old City. Most of the masonry dates from Suleiman the Magnificent but there was probably a gate here in Herod Agrippa's wall.

the Damascus Gate and then running parallel, one in the Tyropoeon valley and the other on its western slopes. The layout is typically Roman, with the plan centered around the cardo maximus and the decumanus, dividing a city into four quarters, each in turn laid out in a grid-iron form modified by the physical topography. A typical layout can still be seen in the northeastern section of the Moslem Quarter.

The original gates in the city walls seem to have been fewer than today. The Madaba map shows only three gates, of which the one to the north, on the site of the present Damascus Gate, is obviously the most important. By Mukaddasi's time, the tally had increased to eight, but the author of *Citez* gives only seven gates, of which three are posterns. By the end of the fifteenth century, Mujir ed-Din enumerates a total of twelve gates. Unfortunately these writers give little indication of the relative importance of these gates. Here *Citez* is more valuable, giving as posterns only, locations which seem to correspond with the

JERUSALEM. Looking west from the Mount of Olives toward the Old City. St. Stephen's Gate may be seen at the left center. Courtesy, Levant Photo Service

Herod's Gate and the Dung Gate of today, neither of which is important. His other four are obviously of greater significance and correspond to the present Jaffa Gate, Damascus Gate, St. Stephen's Gate, and Zion Gate. The latter was of more importance in the past because of the existence of the Latin convent on Mt. Zion, but it can be clearly seen that yet again, the most important gates are in the north. Nomenclature has varied with respect to the gates and care is needed in dealing with old accounts, for instance the St. Stephen's Gate of mediaeval writers is the present Damascus Gate.

The level of the city has been raised over the centuries with the accumulation of rubbish, but as we have seen, the street pattern has tended to persist, even if the present lines are not always identical to the inch with the streets of Aelia. Not only the Madaba map, but also the Copenhagen map of 1180 and The Hague map of 1170 and other old plans show the same pattern persisting. So the skeletal framework of Jerusalem consists of this rectangular pattern of movement. The main north-south street from the Damascus Gate to the Zion and Dung Gates is crossed by a west-east street from the Jaffa Gate to the Haram area. This street finds its continuation eastward in the Via Dolorosa north of the Haram which leaves the city at the present St. Stephen's Gate. Relief gains a say over Roman efficiency, however, in some places, notably in the street which runs down the Tyropoeon valley where the main street of the Biblical city ran.

Beyond the walls, the modern street pattern has settled around the roads to Samaria and Jaffa. In the Arab city, the Nablus Road continues the Suq Khan es-Zeit until it joins, north of St. George's Cathedral, Saladin Street which begins opposite Herod's Gate. A relatively new road, through Gethsemane, provides an east-west zone of movement by running parallel with the northern wall, but outside it, until it links up with the Jaffa Road at Allenby Square.

AREAS OF COMMERCE AND INDUSTRY

In the last chapter we saw the significance of the open square or public meeting place in determining the "core" of the ancient city, and the probability that the central square of Biblical Jerusalem was the Xystus. For the mediaeval and modern city, there is less certainty because after the classical period had passed, with its love of the central forum, the populace seems to have held any public meetings outside the gates. The forum of Aelia was probably in the areas east of the Holy Sepulcher. This would be a central location and the old walls of the Russian Excavations are considered by many to be connected with it. On the Madaba map, a large open square seems to be shown just inside the Damascus Gate where the two north-south streets meet, and considering the importance of this gate (and the tendency of the city to migrate in this direction), this could well have been a public square. On the mediaeval maps a *forum rerum venatium"* is located in the area of the angle formed by the Street of the Chain and the Tariq Bab en Nabi Daud. There seems, anyway, to have been for a long time meeting places around this area between the Haram enclosure and the Citadel. In the modern city, it is difficult to see a central open space, although perhaps the crossroads just outside the Damascus Gate come nearest to it.

There seems to have been a market in operation in the central part of Aelia early on, probably in the northern part of the present Muristan area. A marking which could well represent this is shown on the Madaba map. By Constantine's time an open market seems to have existed in the vicinity of the Holy Sepulcher, according to Eusebius. With the major holy place of the newly "established" Christian church close by, as well as a central location, no doubt the merchants were able to reap rich profits. There was a September fair in existence by the end of the Byzantine era, but of its location there is no certainty, except that a temporary retailing market like this would be likely to find itself just outside one of the main gates. However, from what evidence we have, it appears that the street pattern of Jerusalem and the conveniently central Holy Sepulcher combined to keep the retailing function in a location near the main crossroads and stop a great move towards the northern perimeter. In the Middle Ages this central market location was consolidated. Thus Bernard the Wise tells of a market in front of Charlemagne's hospice, which was just south of the Holy Sepulcher. This was a convenient location as the demand for foodstuffs and other necessaries — as well as for luxuries — from the pilgrims must have been considerable. However, there was some order in the structure of the Central Business District, for Nasir-i-Khusrau, who wrote in the eleventh century, says that "there are in the city numerous artificers and each craft has a separate bazaar," and Mukaddasi in the century before had told of restrictions on where goods could be sold. All this points to a tight control on retailing and a strong tendency for the shopkeepers themselves to group together.

The best description of marketing in mediaeval Jerusalem is found in that most valuable but anonymous work, *Citez de Jherusalem*. It appears that food retailing was more scattered than that of other commodities. So we get corn sold "in a large place on the left hand of the Tower of David," where corn appears to have been stored, suggesting a tendency for migration of retailing to the major western gate. To balance this, however, we find that herbs are sold near the Exchange in the Suq el

Lehhem, the very name suggesting that bread was also sold there. Butchers made a living in the Street of the Temple, and fish appears to have been sold near the Exchange and also at the top of the "covered street," behind the market. Cheese, chickens, eggs and birds were sold here also. Herbs were also sold in the "covered street." The food selling, then, was fairly scattered and extended along the axis from the Tower of David to the Bab el Silsile and around the southern end of the Suq Khan es-Zeit and the Muristan. The Exchange and the gold workers were in this latter place too, the Syrian gold workers on the right hand side of the market and the Latin goldworkers on the left hand side, an interesting ethnic division within a commercial one. Palms were sold in the market and stuffs (textiles) in the "covered street," where they still are sold.

This is the most comprehensive single description of the mediaeval commerce of Jerusalem we have, and with the help of contemporary maps and some other accounts helps to fill in some of the details in the map of Jerusalem at the end of the twelfth century. The advantages for retailers at this period were almost all in favor of a central location with the pilgrim trade centered around the Holy Sepulcher and its surrounding hospices. So the main C.B.D. in the Middle Ages found itself between the Holy Sepulcher and the major crossroads of the Suq Khan es-Zeit and David Street. In fact the Holy Sepulcher exerted such a strong commercial pull on traders, that in the fourteenth century, when Ludolph von Suchem visited the city, the retailers were not averse to moving lock, stock and barrel into that church at Easter and the Eve of the Invention to sell "victuals" to the pilgrims who were locked therein overnight. There must have been keen competition among retailers, but some profit at least probably went back to the church in rents, for we know that some ecclesiastical foundations held property in the suqs as a supplementary source of income. Certainly in the Middle Ages there was a lively trade in this central market, and pilgrims like Theodorich were faced with streets "full of goods for sale."

In the Ottoman period, the main market continued in its central location, but there was also a noticeable movement towards the periphery. To Warburton, the market was confined to one small quarter of the city, probably the southeast part of the Muristan, but Conder tells us that there was a market under David's Tower in the nineteenth century and from Ottoman documents of the sixteenth century we know also that some retailers were selling goods outside the town walls to avoid tax.

This process was encouraged by the plague which swept the city during Edward Robinson's visit and caused the markets to be held at the Damascus and Jaffa Gates. By the same century, a cattle market also existed in the now dry Birket Sultan so one can see some evidence of a dispersal of markets to the northern and western peripheral areas. Inside the city there was definite diversity. Apart from the usual dealers in bread and fruit, the latter in David Street (they still are), there was a cotton bazaar near the Temple area. Provisions continued to be bought and sold in the Holy Sepulcher and the souvenir traders also had a place in front of that church where they sold beads, mother-of-pearl, etc. Souvenirs were also sold in the Latin convent and there were palm sellers in the Harat ed Dabbagh. One interesting feature, however, is that by now the Muristan had ceased to be a market, but according to the map of Aldrich and Symons had become an open field. The main bazaar in the nineteenth century was around the covered street where three parallel streets, arranged "like the nave and aisles of a Church," carried the southern part of the Suq Khan es-Zeit. Formerly the three streets were assigned to different traders but this system became more flexible as time went on, although it can still be seen in modified form today. In the fifteenth century, the western row was used for spices, and its rents and revenues attached to a school built by Saladin; the middle row was the green market — herbs and vegetables; and the third was a market for stuffs.

With the westward growth of the city towards the end of the nineteenth century, the markets seem to have drifted in that direction too. When the British administration took over after the First World War, the retail markets created quite a few headaches. The David Street market, selling vegetables delivered by local villagers, was flourishing, but the newer Jaffa Road market, outside the city walls needed improvement.[1] An attempt had been made before the war to centralize retailing by laying out again the Muristan, but with all the new growth to the north and west a location central to the Old City was becoming somewhat obsolete except for souvenirs and the Muristan even today, remains one of the quietest spots in the city. In modern times this trend has continued, for while many of the suqs flourish, the newer shopping centers are outside. The Nablus Road — Jericho Road area is the C.B.D. for the Arab city and the Jaffa Road — Shlomzion Hamalka Street area is the

---

1 C. R. Ashbee, ed., *Jerusalem 1918-1920*, p. 26.

C.B.D. of the Jewish city. In these places are found the fashion shops, the book shops, the travel agents, the banks, etc. Food and souvenirs are the main items still sold in the Old City. The Suq Khan es-Zeit is still the most popular shopping street with the native Arabs, for food, hardware, and confectionery, while the produce market in David Street still supplies nearly all the hotels in eastern Jerusalem. In the Suq el Kattanin, leading up to the Haram wall, are the metalworkers, and the covered suq still has its sellers of textiles, although butchers have replaced the herb and vegetable sellers. However, the souvenir shops are dominant. These are thickly concentrated in Christian Street and St. Francis Street, in David Street and along the whole route of the Via Dolorosa procession. They are also springing up in the Street of the Chain (Tariq Bab el Silsile), replacing cobblers, carpenters, and metalworkers, as the latter are realizing that this is the route to the Wailing Wall.

Certain special groups of commercial activity have always had special locations. One of these is the financiers and bankers. In the Middle Ages they were firmly entrenched within reach of the pilgrims, and their building, the Exchange, was situated at the southeast corner of the Muristan and there was a Syrian exchange, found in the present Suq Khan es-Zeit. The latter location is interesting, for there is a small group of money chang-

THE VIA DOLOROSA, running north of the Haram enclosure. The school on the right is the site of the Antonia fortress and the street is an example of the many straight roads which reflect the skeleton pattern of Aelia Capitolina.

ers in this street today, just inside the Damascus Gate. Most financiers, as mentioned above, are now in the newer districts outside the city walls.

A very important trade in this city of pilgrims, is the hotel and catering industry. We have little indication of the location of any hospices in the Jerusalem of Biblical times, but for the mediaeval city there is quite a large number of references to hospices. Antoninus Martyr (sixth century) mentions a hospice near the Basilica of the Blessed Mary, which was in the Haram area, holding 3,000 beds. Foreign benefactors often founded hospices for pilgrims, perhaps the most famous such being Charlemagne, who had a hospice for Latin pilgrims built near a Church in honor of St. Mary, close to the Holy Sepulcher. Others sprang up near other holy sites, and there must have been at least one in Bethlehem as one mediaeval traveler stayed there overnight.[2] A hospice sprang up near the royal palace and there was a famous hospice kept by the Knights of St. John in the Muristan area, which held 1,000 pilgrims. The author of *Citez* mentions a hospice in Patriarch Street. For Moslems there was a large khan called al-Wakala, but most of the Christian pilgrims stayed in the convents. The Latin convent was originally found on Mt. Zion but later moved (or rather was forced to move) to a new site in the northeastern part of the city, which was in fact a better location than the older one. Bartlett describes it as the best resting place in the city and even the Protestant Robinson stayed there, and observed that "European visitors, in particular, have ever lodged and still lodge, almost exclusively in the Latin Convent." The Armenian Convent has also been in existence a long time and in the last century was capable of holding 1,000 pilgrims. The Greek Convent is nearer the Holy Sepulcher than the "foreign" ones. The Greek Orthodox Church, being composed largely of native Arab Christians, did not have quite the security problems of the other communities and so could afford to locate nearer the main Christian holy place — the Holy Sepulcher. In the relatively quiet days of the early nineteenth Century, a Coptic Khan was built north of the Birket Hammam al Batrak.

The general trend in the nineteenth Century was, however, to locate hospices more and more outside the city. In 1860, a hospice for Russian pilgrims was founded west of the Old City and a French hospice was also located outside the walls, while the St. George's Cathedral and hostel was built in the angle

---

2 Nasir-i-Khusrau, *Palestine Pilgrim Texts*, p. 53.

ST. GEORGE'S CATHEDRAL. Courtesy, Levant Photo Service

formed by Nablus Road and Saladin Street. Some hospices were still founded in the Old City, though, such as the Anglican Christ Church and the Austrian Hospice, while the Grand New Hotel, one of the first modern hotels in the city, was built inside the walls, opposite the Tower of David. Modern pilgrims use both the hospices in and around Jerusalem and also the modern hotels which are found mainly to the north, west, and on the Mount of Olives. Whereas in former centuries the main requirements for a hospice were security and proximity to the holy sites, the modern hotel is usually sited with regard to the best views, hence the profusion of hotels on the hills to the north and east, with views of Mt. Scopus or the Mount of Olives, and the Intercontinental Hotel on top of the Mount of Olives.

Another trade which has had close connections with the

tourist activity is that of catering. The multitude of cafés and soft-drink sellers in and around the city today have their ancestors in older times as well. In the sixth century, according to Antoninus Martyr, loaves were given to the poor and to pilgrims near the tomb of St. Istius, and the author of *Citez* mentions that food was cooked for pilgrims in a street called Malquisinat. This street was near the Exchange and led to the Holy Sepulcher. The cafés and soft-drink stalls are fairly ubiquitous, and do a good trade in the more out-of-the-way places such as the top of the Mount of Olives and Bethany.

With regard to the location of industrial activity, there is not much information in the pilgrim accounts, and as most industries are of the small-scale family variety, the visitor to the city, even today, often overlooks them. Leather work and textiles are an old group of industries, serving rather the local populace than the tourist industry direct. Tanning has been established in the city for many centuries and is mentioned frequently in pilgrim accounts because of the habit which the Moslems had of locating tanners' workshops near Christian holy sites, thus creating a most obnoxious smell. The Tarik Bab el Amud, which was the name given to the northern part of the Suq Khan es-Zeit, was also called the "Tannery" at one time, and maybe there were tanners' works here. It was a complaint of many later pilgrims that the tannery near the Pool of Siloam was obnoxious, although this location may well have been justified on the grounds that here there was plenty of water. Even as late as the nineteenth century there was a foul-smelling tannery in front of the Holy Sepulcher, noticed by Robinson. Weaving was practiced in the Place of Scourging according to Maundrell and later there was a weaving center in the Suq el Kattanin. Pottery manufacture, as we have seen, is an old industry in Jerusalem, and today is quite flourishing, making objects for the tourist industry as well as for household use. The "Palestine Potteries" is a well known factory on the Nablus Road, just opposite the Mandelbaum gate. Other industries in the city have included carpentry and furniture manufacture, which are concentrated today near the Bab el Jadid in the northwest corner of the city and wood and metal workshops are found in the Tariq Bab el Nabi Daud and the Streets el Kattanin and Silsile. Souvenir manufacture is found in many places, there being a large workshop in the western section of the Via Dolorosa, although a large amount of the supply for the souvenir retailers comes from Bethlehem, where the industry has been established since the end of the Middle Ages.

AREAS OF ADMINISTRATION

The importance played by royal palaces and fortresses in Biblical Jerusalem seems not to have been repeated after the founding of the new city, and little mention is made in contemporary accounts of either administrative places or military strongpoints. It seems that in general the Citadel of David's Tower remained the main government stronghold, although the old Antonia was also used as a barracks. The legionary headquarters of Aelia were south of the Citadel and this appears to have remained the important military center throughout the city's history. It does not appear strongly on the Madaba Map, perhaps because times were peaceful enough not to warrant its importance, but appears on mediaeval maps as the distinctive fortress in the city. In Turkish times, there was a barracks both here and also in the Antonia fortress, in order to guard both sides of the city. With regard to the civilian government, a building is shown on the Madaba map near the southern end of the Tarik Bab al Nabi Daud which could be a town hall or something similar. The only period in which administrative and military buildings really spread over the city was under the Crusaders. Godfrey de Bouillon held his first courts in the Al Aqsa mosque, which later became the headquarters of the Knights Templar after the king moved to a new residence in David's Tower. The Knights of St. John, the other famous military order, had their headquarters in the Muristan area, just south of the Holy Sepulcher, while another royal palace existed west of that Church probably on the site of the present Greek Patriarchate. For most of the time, from its founding in A.D. 132 to the time of the British Mandate, Jerusalem was not a national capital, and so the barracks and the administrative buildings were of a diminutive nature, but after the entry of the British, national government offices were built in the Jaffa Road and civic administration was carried on from a building just north of the Jaffa Gate. Administrative activity has not had any great influence on modern Jerusalem, although in the new Jewish city, the Knesset building and the many new ministries springing up are beginning to influence the land use.

AGRICULTURAL AREAS

The agricultural and gardening activity in and around the city has been concentrated, as in Biblical times, in the valleys. The area immediately below the Pool of Siloam appears to have benefited very much from overflow water and flourished throughout the mediaeval period. Joannas Phocas (twelfth century), noticed that the pool overflowed and watered the surrounding countryside, supporting meadows and trees, while Nasir-i-Khusrau (11th Century) saw the "Ain Silwan" flow to a village and water gardens. The same patch of ground was also irrigated from Siloam in the nineteenth century and at the beginning of the present century there was a cauliflower patch there. There is also some evidence that there was a fish pond south of the pool in the Middle Ages. Some cultivation around Job's Well seems to have been carried on in the last century, including an olive grove. Further up the Kidron there were other gardens. The Virgin's Fountain watered gardens in the Middle Ages, probably those of the hospice of Charlemagne which was supplied with food direct from its own fields. Gethsemane appears to have continued to delight pilgrims with its green luxuriance. The Bordeaux Pilgrim noticed vineyards and palm trees in this stretch of the Kidron and there was once a fig tree here which was pointed out to pilgrims as the one where Judas hanged himself. The garden is frequently mentioned in mediaeval accounts, including those by Arab writers. Maundrell noticed its olive trees, the produce of which was exported to Spain, but to Warburton it was "only a small grove." It is pretty clear, however, that the Kidron Valley with its ease of access to the city and better water supply than the Hinnom, was the main vegetable garden for Jerusalem until the city grew too large to be supplied just from such a convenient source. The Hinnom Valley was widely used for cemeteries in the Christian era, in which fruit trees were cultivated. Olives, lentils and other trees were grown here in Ottoman times, and it seems that corn was grown as well. Flocks of sheep and goats graze its slopes and in the lower reaches it still presents a very pleasant appearance. Of the hills, much the same pattern continued as in Biblical times. The rising ground to the north of Jerusalem, despite good soil, has never until recent decades had enough water to develop strong agricultural interests and the hills around the city have generally been given over to tree cultivation, grazing and cemeteries. The seventh-century writer Arculfus, after remarking on the existence of olives east of Jerusalem, comments that there were few trees on Olivet, except vines and olives, but wheat and barley flourished. His explanation for this, is that the soil is not favorable for trees but is good for grass and flowers. Theodorich gives the hill more lavish praise, and according to him it "abounds in fruit of all kinds." It rather seems as if the flourishing commerce of Jerusalem in Byzantine and early

Arab times encouraged fairly intense cultivation of the Mount of Olives, but by the time we arrive at the Ottoman period, comments are less complimentary and the hill seems to have contained a few old trees with flocks grazing among them. One area cultivated in Byzantine and mediaeval times was the open land south of the city walls where once stood the cities of Nehemiah and the Herods. Mt. Zion and the lower Tyropoeon in particular, seem to have been the scene of growing vegetables on many occasions, although in the last century the cultivation was less intense and the main crops were olives and corn, with goats and sheep grazing among them. More intense vegetable cultivation increased in this century, and a large number of houses with gardens attached have been constructed since the last World War, although there are still many patches of waste, especially along the old armistice line.

Inside the city, there were many parks and gardens in the Middle Ages. Felix Fabri found a garden in the old palace of the Crusader kings and, according to Suriano, the Birket Israel was used as a garden. It was in fact a usual sight in cities of the Arab world in mediaeval times to find parks and gardens within the walls, and reports of such in Antioch and Damascus as well as at Jerusalem are common. However, as we have seen, the Ottoman period brought a decline in commerce and trade and also in land usage to the city. The cultivated area around the city retracted back to the immediate valleys, and much waste and open space (uncultivated) appeared within the city walls. The northeast part of the city was particularly empty in the nineteenth century and consisted according to Ritter of "mere fields and a hill scantily covered with houses." It still has patches of waste just inside Herod's Gate. The northwest corner was empty and according to Hanauer was sown with grain, while in the Jewish Quarter, the part next to the southwest corner of the Haram was under the plough. The emptiness of the city in the early part of the last century was such that George Williams remarked that the traveler "no sooner enters the city than desolation stares him in the face."

AREAS OF RESIDENCE

The large area in any city taken up by residential building is, as seen in the last chapter, considerably greater than that occupied by commerce and industry. In the case of Jerusalem, we have seen that the residential areas have tended to move to the north and west in response to economic and also social pressures, and at many periods of the city's history there has been a large number of houses outside the walls. So here the residential areas within the Old City will be differentiated from the suburbs which from time to time have developed in extramural locations. The colony of Aelia was largely confined to its walls, which covered a considerably smaller area than the city of Herod Agrippa. The residential areas of the city probably lay in the north and south, separated by the commercial and cultural "core" area in the center. In Byzantine times, however, with the great influx of population brought about by the first Christian pilgrim "boom," residential areas developed outside the city walls again. Many remains of buildings dating from this era have been found to the north and south of the city, and churches particularly sprang up with attendant suburban settlement around them. To the north a number of Byzantine remains have been found which show of the spread in this direction, and on the hills of Zion and Ophel there must have been a considerable population from the remains which have been found. The hill of Mt. Zion was walled round probably by the Empress Eudoxia, and formed a new suburb attached to the city, while there seems to have been some spread onto the Mount of Olives. Within the Old City, there was a denser settlement. After the Arab conquest, the Old City remained alone and there seems to have been little suburban growth beyond the walls. Security was never very great even in the stern days of Turkish rule and it was generally safer for a citizen to build his house within the walls. Security was also a major factor in the development of the ethnic quarters which are so characteristic of Jerusalem. The four quarters of the present Old City have a long history, although they have not always been in the same places as today. Neither must they be regarded as inflexible divisions, for Moslems and Christians can often be found living in the "wrong" quarters. Yet the factors operating to drive the different groups apart have been strong. We have already seen how in ancient times, the traders often lived and worked in separate quarters, especially those who were foreigners, in order to have mutual fellowship and security. In the much more cosmopolitan Jerusalem of the Middle Ages, the tendency for men of the same nationality or religion to group together was even stronger. Life was often cheap, and a Christian living alone surrounded by Moslem neighbors might be the subject not only of scorn and ridicule, but of physical violence as well. However, if all the Christians or Jews grouped themselves together, they could present a much more solid face to the world, and a man was assured that his immediate neighbors at least were friendly. The process can be seen in Suriano's account of his stay in the Holy Land in charge of the Latin monastery, when he attempted to buy up the land around it in order that the monks could live in peace. In fact he gives a very good picture of the divisions of the city in the fifteenth century. The Latins were still on Mt. Zion, although they were now in somewhat cramped quarters, as much of their land had been taken away from them. The Greek Orthodox community lived, it appears, around the Holy Sepulcher. There was no love lost between the various Christian communities, for Suriano says of the Greeks that they "are our worst and atrocious enemies." The Georgians were then strong in the city, for they had three monasteries, one by the Holy Sepulcher, and were described by Suriano as "the worst heretics." The Armenians appear to have lived then in approximately the same Armenian Quarter which we know today, centered around their cathedral and convent of St. James. They, too, were not universally liked, for while Suriano says of them that "they love us cordially," they were apparently the "deadly enemies of the Greeks and Georgians." The Syrian Orthodox community was then, as today, few in numbers and seem to have owned the same property, i.e. a part of the Holy Sepulcher and their church in the northeastern part of the Armenian Quarter. The Abyssinians, "heretics of the worst kind," lived in the Holy Sepulcher and in David's penance place. Other groups in the city included the Nestorians, the Copts, the Jacobites, and groups called the "Essenes," the "Assassins" and the "Sadducees". It seems that the multitude of Christian groups each feared each other as much as the Moslems, for each had their own little quarters huddled around their churches and convents. The distinction between the Armenian and the Christian Quarters, puzzling to many people, is probably explained by the quarrels between the Armenians and the Greeks. After the Ottoman conquest and the rebuilding of the southern wall of the city on the present line, the Sultan turned the Franciscans out of their quarter on Mt. Zion, and gave them a place in the Christian Quarter, where they have been ever since, with their hospice, the Casa Nova, patriarchate, seminary, and other buildings, forming a neat block in the extreme northeast of the Old City, which until the New Gate was built in the last century, was a quiet backwater.

The Moslems have been the dominant group in the city since the end of the Crusader period and have lived all over the

NEW BUILDINGS. In this section north of the Old City is a hotel (center) and the police station (left).

city. However, as the Christian groups bought up their parcels of land to form their quarters, the Moslems have been left largely in the northeast area and the district immediately west of the northern half of the Haram walls. They have been almost entirely of the Sunni sect, but the presence of some Shi'as does not seem to have caused the strife which we have seen exist between the Christian groups. The Jews, who have been living in quarters or ghettos throughout the world for many centuries, seem in the early Middle Ages to have lived in the northeastern part of the city, which was known in the western world as the Juiverie. Later they moved to the area southwest of the Haram where they built their synagogues and schools and lived — if one is to believe many accounts — a wretched existence, in great poverty and relying on foreign aid.

The residential developments in Jerusalem of the last hundred years have been perhaps the most significant factor in the city's urban geography. There have been changes inside the walls and great changes outside. At present we have really two cities, one Jewish with new suburbs of blocks of flats; the other consists of the Old City within the walls, still very much a Turkish provincial town, with a pleasant suburban growth of detached houses to the north. There has also been a less pleasant, and rather unplanned, urban sprawl to the south of the city. Inside the Old City, the quarters still remain much the same, except that since 1948, the Jewish Quarter has lain largely empty. The Christian Quarter consists of so many public buildings — hospices, convents, churches, etc. — that one wonders whether it can still be called residential, but the Armenian and Moslem Quarters still consist largely of private houses. On the Arab side of the city, suburban growth has extended generally east of the Saladin Street and across the Wadi El Joz, which is the name given to the upper Kidron with new communities of Bab Ezahirah Wadi El Joz and Sheik Jarrah. The development was spearheaded by the construction of the St. George's Compound and the American Colony, but development proceeded swiftly after 1948 when both here and on the Mount of Olives there was much building of houses to accommodate people working in the now booming tourist industry. The developments in and around the village of Silwan have been more haphazard and house largely the poorer members of the populace.

It is the development to the west that has been the most spectacular aspect of suburban growth in Jerusalem. This area remained largely undeveloped until the second half of the last century. The Russian Compound, described by Wilson and Warren as an "unsightly pile," led this development and the German "Temple" community settled near the railway station. This station provided great impetus for growth on this side of the city and with the pressures of Jewish immigration, new settlements were founded in the few decades just before the First World War to house Jews. Montefiore's project is one famous example, calling itself Yemin Moshe after its founder. It soon vied with the Jewish Quarter within the Old City as a symbol of the orthodox. Since the British took over administration, and more so since the western part of the city has been in Israel, this rapid suburban development along the road to Jaffa has been pronounced. Israeli planners have tried to build the more western suburbs on the ridges of high ground leaving the valleys open. As most of the housing has been in the form of blocks of flats, this need for open space has been all the more urgent. Parks have been laid out to make the western suburbs pleasant to live in and the city has reached so far west that Beit Ha Kerem is now an outer dormitory.

POINTS OF RELIGIOUS ACTIVITY

Finally, mention must be made of the points of religious activity which are so important in this holy city. The main shrines have already been dealt with in Chapter 5, but it remains to tie them in with the other aspects of the urban geography of the city. The main holy sites are within the Old City, to the south of it, and to the east of it. It is rather interesting that this should be so, because it runs counter to the pronounced tendency for the city to develop to the north and west. Apart from the Garden Tomb and the Tombs of the Kings, there are practically no holy sites of any of the major faiths, in these directions. However, it must not be assumed that therefore the location of holy sites has had no influence on the growth of the city at all.

In Biblical times, we noticed that the Temple had a considerable influence in attracting settlement and commerce around it, and in Byzantine times the holy sites on the Mount of Olives and Mt. Zion seemed to spearhead a residential movement onto these hills. Movement north and west has probably been influenced more by commercial considerations and the availability of flat land for building, but that does not prove that the holy sites exerted no pull at all. For most of the Middle Ages and the Ottoman period, the holy sites were inside the Old City. Of those on the Mt. of Olives, most were either in ruins or not in existence at all until the last century. The Church of the Agony, the Russian Church, the Dominus Flevit Church, and the Paternoster Church are all recent buildings, even if they are on ancient sites. It is significant that in recent years, with greater personal security as well as a vastly increased tourist trade, the Mount of Olives has once again been built upon by private dwellers, while strict planning has kept new building down in the Gethsemane area and on the western slopes of the mount.[3]

It is interesting to notice how pilgrim activity has changed over the centuries. In the Byzantine times, it was the Mount of Olives, with the place of Ascension particularly which attracted the pilgrims. The Bordeaux Pilgrim also visited Zion and the Pool of Siloam. The rest of the sites were inside the walls, namely the Holy Sepulcher and Golgotha, the Pool of Bethesda and the Tower of David. Such a small number of sites is to be compared with accounts of the Middle Ages, when we have sites for the birth, death, and burial of Mary, the house of the Last Supper, the house of St. John, the tombs of David and Solomon, the place where Judas hanged himself, the fig tree which Jesus cursed, etc. Thus by the end of the Middle Ages there was a considerable dispersion of pilgrim activity, with many sites now lost or deemed unnecessary in a less credulous

3 H. Kendall, *Jerusalem City Plan* (1948).

age. By the nineteenth century, the number of sites had slumped and many former churches were in ruins. Now the number has stabilized itself somewhat and those sites with a good view of the city or the surrounding countryside, or with ruins visible are the most popular. This brings more tourist activity to the Mount of Olives and the sites in the northeast of the Old City. The Holy Sepulcher, though still revered by thousands of adherents to the Eastern churches and by many Roman Catholics, has lost much of its attraction for the twentieth Century tourist/pilgrim. So the dispersal of business and suburbia outwards to the north and west has been paralleled by a dispersion of the tourist industry east and south. If present building trends continue, there will be a "green belt" from the Wadi Joz round the Old City to Yemin Moshe, and including the western slopes of the Mount of Olives, separating the present town from the eastern suburbs which are developing beyond the Mount of Olives to Bethany and around the Mount of Offence. It is to preserve this Pilgrim Belt that much of the planning of eastern Jerusalem must be directed.

BIBLIOGRAPHY

This bibliography is not exhaustive but is intended as a guide to further reading and deeper study. For works prior to 1870 a useful bibliographical reference is R. Rohricht, *Bibliotheca Geographica Palaestinae*, Berlin, 1890. The most useful journals in the field are:

Palestine Exploration Quarterly (PEQ)
Annual & Bulletin of the American Schools of Oriental Research (AASOR)
Israel Exploration Journal (IEJ)
Journal of Near Eastern Studies (JNES)
Journal of Royal Central Asian Society (JRCAS)
Revue Biblique (RB)
Eretz Israel (EI)
Ariel
Quarterly of Department of Antiquities of Palestine (QDAP)
Zeitschrift des Deutsche Palaestina Vereins (ZDPV)

MIDDLE EAST (GENERAL)

G. B. Cressey, *Crossroads: Land and Life of Southwest Asia.* Chicago, 1960.

W. B. Fisher, *The Middle East.* London, 1963 (5th ed.).

G. E. Kirk, *A Short History of the Middle East.* London, 1964.

PALESTINE (GENERAL)

G. A. Smith, *The Historical Geography of the Holy Land.* London, 1894.

E. Orni and E. Efrat, *Geography of Israel.* Jerusalem, 1966.
The best modern general textbook.

D. Baly, *The Geography of the Bible.* London, 1957.

Y. Aharoni, *The Land of the Bible.* London, 1967.

Sir C. Warren and C. R. Conder, *The Survey of Western Palestine.* London, 1884.

M. Avi-Yonah, *The Holy Land from the Persian to the Arab Conquest.* Grand Rapids, 1966.

G. Le Strange, *Palestine under the Moslems.* Beirut, 1965.
Reprint from 1890 edition. Gives extracts from Arab travelers of the Middle Ages arranged topographically. Other details of Arab sources are given in:

A. -S. Marmardji, *Textes Geographiques Arabes sur la Palestine.* Paris, 1951.
Translations of accounts (mainly European) are given in Palestine Pilgrim Texts series, published in London in the 1880's.
On cartographic sources see:

I. W. J. Hopkins, "Maps and Plans of Bible Lands." *Evangelical Quarterly,* Vol. XL. No. 1, 1968.

----------, "Nineteenth Century Maps of Palestine." *Imago Mundi.* Vol. XXII, 1968.

JERUSALEM (GENERAL)

G. A. Smith, *Jerusalem* (2 vols.). London, 1907.

C. Wilson and C. Warren, *The Recovery of Jerusalem.* London, 1871.

W. Besant and E. H. Palmer, *Jerusalem: The City of Herod and Saladin.* London, 1908.

L. H. Vincent, *Jerusalem: recherches en topographie, d'archeologie et d'histoire.* Paris, 1912-26.

L. H. Vincent and A. M. Steve, *Jerusalem de l'ancien Testament.* Paris, 1956.

J. Simons, *Jerusalem in the Old Testament.* Leiden, 1952.

M. Join-Lambert, *Jerusalem.* London, 1958.

K. M. Kenyon, *Jerusalem.* London, 1969.
Mainly Biblical city.

M. Avi-Yonah, *Sepher Yerushalaim.* Jerusalem, 1956.

Z. Vilnay, *Yerushalaim Hair Haatikah.* Jerusalem, 1967.

E. Efrat, *Yerushalaim ve Haperutzdor.* Jerusalem, 1967.
The last three excellent works are in Hebrew.

A. L. Tibawi, *Jerusalem: Its Place in Islam and Arab History.* Beirut, 1969.

C. F. Pfeiffer, *Jerusalem Through the Ages.* Grand Rapids, 1967.

I. A. Abbady, *Jerusalem Economy.* Jerusalem, 1950.

G. H. Dalman, *Jerusalem und sein Gelaende.* Guetersloh, 1930.

H. Kendall, *Jerusalem City Plan.* London, 1948.

GEOLOGY, CLIMATE AND WATER SUPPLY

M. Blanckenhorn, "Geologie der naheren Umgebung von Jerusalem." *ZDVP.* Vol. 28, 1905.

M. Avnimelech, "Geological Influences on the Development of Jerusalem." *BASOR*, Feb., 1966.

N. Rosenau, "One Hundred Years of Rainfall in Jerusalem." *IEJ.* Vol 5. 1955.

W. T. Massey, "The Jerusalem Water Supply." *PEQ*, 1918.

E. W. G. Masterman, "The Pool of Bethesda." *PEQ*, 1921.

ECONOMY AND SOCIETY

E. Efrat, "The Hinterland of the New City of Jerusalem and its Economic Significance." *Economic Geography.* Vol. 40, 1964.

Hashemite Kingdom of Jordan — Statistical Handbook: 1964.

I. W. J. Hopkins, *Tourism in Jerusalem.* Report for the Ministry of Tourism, Israel. Durham, 1969.

O. Schmelz, "Development of the Jewish Population of Jerusalem During the Last Hundred Years." *Jewish Journal of Sociology.* 1957.

HOLY SITES AND SITES OF EXCAVATIONS

E. A. Moore, *The Ancient Churches of Old Jerusalem.* Beirut, 1961.

L. H. Vincent and F. M. Abel, *Jerusalem Nouvelle.* Paris, 1926.

J. Hanauer, *Walks about Jerusalem.* London, 1910.

G. T. Jahshan and M. A. Jahshan, *Guide to the West Bank of Jordan.* Jerusalem, 1965.

E. Hoade, *Jerusalem and its Environs.* Jerusalem, 1964.

S. Perowne, *Jerusalem.*
The three books listed above are tourist guidebooks.

L. H. Vincent, *Jerusalem Sous Terre.* Paris, 1911.

R. Weill, *La Cite de David.* Paris, 1920 and 1947.

F. J. Bliss and Dickie, *Excavations at Jerusalem 1894-97.* London, 1898.

J. W. Crowfoot and G. N. Fitzgerald, "Excavations in the Tyropoeon Valley, Jerusalem." *Annual of Palestine Exploration Fund.* Vol. V. London, 1929.

K. M. Kenyon, *Jerusalem.*

----------, "Excavations in Jerusalem." *PEQ,* 1961-8.

R. A. S. Macalister and J. G. Duncan, "Excavations on the Hill of Ophel, Jerusalem." *Annual of Palestine Exploration Fund.* Vol. IV. London, 1926.

R. W. Hamilton, "Excavations Against the North Wall." *QDAP,* 1944.

C. W. Wilson, *Golgotha and the Holy Sepulchre.* London, 1906.

C. M. Watson, *Golgotha and the Holy Sepulchre.* London, 1918.

R. A. S. Macalister, "The 'Garden Tomb.' " *PEQ,* 1907.

N. P. Clarke, "The Four North Walls of Jerusalem." *PEQ,* 1944.

A. Parrot, *The Temple of Jerusalem.* London, 1957.

Aref el-Aref, "The Dome of the Rock and Al-Aqsa Mosque." *Ariel.* No. 23, 1969.

H. W. Trusen, "Geschichte von Gethsemane." *ZDPV,* XXXIII. 1910.

G. A. Barton, "The Tombs of the Judges." *Journal of Biblical Literature.* XXII, 1903.

W. Simpson, "The Royal Caverns or Quarries." *PEQ,* 1870.

G. Schick, "Plan of Jeremiah's Grotto." *PEQ,* 1902.

J. Germer-Durand, "La maison de Caiphe et l'eglise S. Pierre." *RB,* 1914.

L. H. Vincent, "L'Antonia et le Pretoire." *RB,* 1933.

C. N. Johns, "Excavations at the Citadel of Jerusalem." *QDAP.* 1936, and *PEQ,* 1940.

A. W. Crawley-Boevey, "The Damascus Gate or Bab el-Amud." *PEQ,* 1912.

J. Wilkinson, *The Stations of the Cross in Jerusalem.* Jerusalem, 1963.

G. H. Dalman, *Sacred Sites and Ways.* London, 1935.

MISCELLANEOUS

D. E. Sopher, *The Geography of Religions.* New Jersey, 1967.

A. S. Atiyeh, *A History of Eastern Christianity.* London, 1968.

P. Birot and J. Dresch, *La Mediterranee et le Moyen Orient.* Paris, 1956.

T. F. O'Dea, *The Sociology of Religion.* New Jersey, 1966.

E. Robinson, *Biblical Researches in Palestine.* London, 1867.

J. Beaujeu-Garnier and G. Chabot, *Urban Geography.* London, 1967.

INDEX OF SCRIPTURE REFERENCES

156

GENERAL INDEX

Aelia Capitolina, 80, 103, 112, 116-117, 122, 132, *139*, 143, 146
Agriculture, 20, 25, 27, 37-38, 59-62
  Areas of, 127-129, 143-145
Anathoth, 20
Arab settlements, 14, 32, 90, 109-113 *113*, 117, 133, 140, 146-149
Area of city, 95-114
  during Arab era, 105-107
  during Byzantine era, 104
  during Christian era, 100
  during Crusader era, 105-107
  during Davidic era, 96
  during Hellenistic era, 99-100
  during Modern era, 109-111
  during Ottoman era, 108-109
  during post-Exilic era, 98
  during pre-Davidic era, 96
  during pre-Exilic era, 98
  during Roman era, 100
Armenian Quarter, 36, 92, 113, 140, 147
Ashqelon, 26
Axes of Jerusalem, 16-27
  Eastern axis, 27
  Northern axis, 18-22
  Southern axis, 22-25
  Western axis, 25-26

Beroth, 20
Bethany, 27, 60, 61, 87, 111, 142, 151
Bethel, 21
Bethlehem, 16, 22-25, *23*, *24*, 56, 60-61, *62*, 64, 82, 140, 142

Beth Shemesh, 26
Bezetha Hill, 32, 34

Calvary, *65*. *See also* Gordon's Calvary, Golgotha
Christian settlements, 20, 22, 36, 140, 146-149
Church of All Nations, 93-94
Church of the Ascension, 87, 94
Church of the Redeemer, 90
Climate, 14, 25, 27-44
  Rainfall, 25, 27, 37, 38, 41-43, 45-46
  Rain shadow, 42-43
  Snowfall, 43
  Temperature, 43-44
Coastal plain, 14
Commerce
  Areas of, 121-125, 130, 135-142
  Center of, 110
Crusades, 81-82

David's Tower (*or* Citadel), 68, 100, 122, 123, 128, 129, 136-137, 143, 150
Dome of the Ascension, 79
Dome of the Rock, 34, 65, 78, 86, 87, 130

Earthquakes, 31-32
Economy of Jerusalem 58-72. *See also* Agriculture, Commerce, Financial activity, Government activity, Industry, Jerusalem — as market place, — as pilgrim/tourist center, — as religious center, Markets, Retail
Emmaus, 26